Last Wishes

A HANDBOOK TO GUIDE YOUR SURVIVORS

Last Wishes

A HANDBOOK TO GUIDE YOUR SURVIVORS

LUCINDA PAGE KNOX, M.S.W.
MICHAEL D. KNOX, Ph.D.

AUTHORS' NOTE

We welcome all reader comments and suggestions. Please send any correspondence to us through our publisher.

Lucinda and Michael Knox
Ulysses Press
P.O. Box 3440
Berkeley, California 94703-3440

Published by: Ulysses Press
          P.O. Box 3440
          Berkeley, California 94703

Library of Congress Catalog Card Number: 94-61744

ISBN: 1-56975-024-6

Printed in the USA by Patterson Printing

10 9 8 7 6 5 4 3 2 1

1. Funeral—Memorial—Workbooks—Handbooks, manuals
2. Death—Dying

Managing Editor: Claire Chun
Editor: Joanna Pearlman
Project Director: Jennifer Wilkoff
Indexer: Sayre Van Young
Proofreaders: Lee Micheaux, Mark Rosen
Cover photograph: Robert Holmes
Cover design: DesignWorks
Color separation: ProScan

Distributed in the United States by Publishers Group West and in Canada by Raincoast Books.

Last Wishes is dedicated to our parents:
Mary L. Knox, Harold L. Knox, Shirley J. Page,
and to the memory of Judge John S. Page.

ACKNOWLEDGMENTS

We would like to thank the many family members, friends, and colleagues who took time to read our manuscript and make suggestions, many of which have been incorporated into the final version of this book. We are grateful to our sons John and James for their patience and understanding during this project.

THE LAST WISHES OF

_____

(fill in your name)

We recommend that you review the contents of *Last Wishes* once a year with your spouse, partner, friend, or whoever will be carrying out your wishes. Let that person know where to locate the book. Use a pencil for items that may change so that they may be revised when necessary. Having current financial and legal information readily available will spare your survivors much anxiety and confusion. A periodic review will ensure that your wishes are up to date. Note each review and/or revision date below. This will indicate that all of your wishes are current and accurate as of that date.

Date Prepared _____

Dates Reviewed/Revised

Date _____ Initials _____   Date _____ Initials _____

Date _____ Initials _____   Date _____ Initials _____

Date _____ Initials _____   Date _____ Initials _____

Date _____ Initials _____   Date _____ Initials _____

Date _____ Initials _____   Date _____ Initials _____

Date _____ Initials _____   Date _____ Initials _____

Date _____ Initials _____   Date _____ Initials _____

Date _____ Initials _____   Date _____ Initials _____

Date _____ Initials _____   Date _____ Initials _____

Date _____ Initials _____   Date _____ Initials _____

Date _____ Initials _____   Date _____ Initials _____

Date _____ Initials _____   Date _____ Initials _____

TABLE OF CONTENTS

*L̶ife is half-
spent before we know
what it is.*

George Herbert

FOREWORD

Most of us plan very carefully for the major events of life so they come out just the way we want them to, yet we try hard *not* to think about the final climactic event—our death.

We labor over our wedding vows, but leave the epitaph on our gravestone for others to write. We agonize over whom to invite to birthday parties and anniversary celebrations, but ignore the guest list for our funeral service. We carefully arrange for the care of our pets when we travel, but make no provisions for their welfare after we die. When it comes to planning our funerals and settling our affairs, we leave the decision, the work—and the outcome—to others.

It's true that many of us do write wills, and some of us go so far as to pick—even pay for—a cemetery plot. But how many people do you know who selected the music to be played at their funeral, or left a personal message to be read at their memorial service? If these ideas sound strange, even morbid, to you, think for a moment how they might benefit your survivors.

Putting your last wishes down on paper lifts a major burden from the shoulders of those you leave behind. After all, if you don't deal with these issues, your loved ones and friends will have to do it for you.

But there's an even more important reason to define your last wishes now: It sends a parting message of love and consideration to your survivors. It's a unique way of saying, "Don't worry about me; I'll be okay. Just take care of yourselves for me." It will also help them to know that *you* were able to confront the issues that *they* will find so difficult to face.

If you're still feeling a little nervous about the idea of planning ahead for death—your death—take a few minutes now to browse through the chapters of this book. I think you'll be pleasantly surprised at how many positive feelings reading *Last Wishes* will evoke, especially as you reflect on the story of your life and the people you care about.

When you are ready, begin filling out the workbook. That will give you the peace of mind that comes from preparing ahead of time for this important event. It will also bring comfort to your loved ones and friends, who will know that they are carrying out your last wishes in just the way you would have wanted.

Arthur Ulene, M.D.

Chapter

I

INTRODUCTION

INTRODUCTION

If you died tomorrow, would your survivors be able to find your will? Could they locate all other necessary documents in order to prepare an accurate and detailed obituary? Would they know your funeral and burial preferences? Would they know where to find the addresses and phone numbers of your friends and the organizations to which you belong, a summary of your assets, or your life insurance policies?

More than 2 million people die each year in the United States. Most die unexpectedly without leaving specific written instructions for their survivors. This creates difficulties for relatives and friends who must make sudden, painful decisions about funeral and burial details. How much easier it would be to know the preferences of the deceased. And—in many instances—how differently the deceased would have staged his or her own funeral! A common observation at many funerals is that "He/she wouldn't have wanted it this way."

You *can* have it your way. We recognize that talking about death and funeral arrangements is difficult for all concerned, so *Last Wishes* allows you to put your thoughts down on paper. You can review the book later with family members or friends, ask that they read it, or simply notify a close friend of the existence and location of *Last Wishes* so that he/she will know where to look at the time of your death.

Last Wishes is a guide that will benefit both you and your survivors. You can have peace of mind knowing that your funeral and burial instructions are contained in this book. There are also chapters pertaining to legal and financial information, personal history, and persons and organizations you wish contacted after your death. *Last Wishes* also includes a place where you can list your financial accounts, insurance policies, and major assets. Your survivors will then know exactly how you want the details of your death to be handled, how to locate all of your important documents, what assets you own, and how you want small, personal items to be distributed.

And therefore never send to know for whom the bell tolls; it tolls for thee.

John Donne

In *Last Wishes* you can record, for example, the type of funeral or memorial service you desire; how you want your remains to be disposed; and where you would like to be buried—or entombed—or scattered. You can write your own obituary and choose the music to be played during your service. You are even encouraged to design your own headstone!

Last Wishes will also remind you of other important tasks you may want to complete, such as preparing a will, completing organ donor forms, joining a memorial society, choosing a funeral home, or purchasing a burial plot.

Readers who undertake this task in good health and who do not face imminent death may wish to write their choices in pencil and update *Last Wishes* as information and preferences change. Do not try to complete the book in one sitting, but fill it in gradually as you have the time.

For those who are unable or who do not wish to go through the entire book, please read our "Guide to Priority Chapters," page 5. We have listed what we feel are the most important sections to be completed.

There is also a "Guide for Survivors," page 6, which refers survivors to the information that they will need immediately following your death in order to make funeral/memorial service, burial, and other arrangements.

We hope that those of you who complete *Last Wishes* as you near death can appreciate this opportunity to review your life, document your plans, and thereby extend your individualism and autonomy. Taking charge of the final details can have a positive impact on how others remember you and can help your loved ones to better cope with your death. Your ability to make decisions in this book may enhance your autonomy at a time when other aspects of your life may seem out of your control.

This is not meant to be a gloomy, morbid exercise. But, as Moliere wrote, "We only die once, and for such a long time!" You may as well state exactly how you wish this "once in a lifetime" occasion to be handled. Simply fill in the blanks, update as needed, and tell your family or friends where this book is located. It may also be a good idea to copy pertinent information from this book to keep on file with your attorney and at the funeral home of your choice.

The information that you include in *Last Wishes* should be reviewed periodically. Use a pencil for items that may change so that they may be revised when necessary. Having current financial and legal information readily available will spare your survivors much anxiety and confusion. Note each review date on page vii. This will indicate that all of your wishes are current and accurate as of that date. We recommend that you review the contents of *Last Wishes* once a year with your spouse, partner, friend, or whoever will be carrying out your wishes.

There are other books that go into greater detail regarding all aspects of death, funerals, and legal and financial issues. You will be referred to examples of these in the Appendix. We encourage you to do further reading on these topics before you make your final decisions. The Appendix also includes sample obituaries and lists of organizations and readings that offer practical advice, information, and solace.

We hope that your work in *Last Wishes* will result in an individualized, creative, and meaningful memorial and that the information you record in this book will provide valued memories for those who mourn your death.

NOTE: Last Wishes *is not intended to replace a will, living will, or other legal documents. Please seek legal advice as you organize your estate.*

GUIDE TO PRIORITY CHAPTERS

You may not have the time, health, energy, or inclination to complete this entire book. Please don't let the size and scope of the chapters overwhelm you. We recommend that the following sections be given first priority; the information you include here will be most important if you are suddenly incapacitated and will also be necessary for your survivors to have immediately following your death.

You may also wish to refer to some of the legal and financial books listed in the Appendix and to browse through the quotes at the end of the book.

GUIDE FOR SURVIVORS

Immediately following the death of your loved one, you will need certain information in order to plan for the disposition of his or her body, the funeral and/or memorial service, and the obituary. You will also want to notify family members and friends.

We recommend that you look through the following chapters and sub-headings first, in the order given.

L̸ove is as strong as death.

Solomon

Also, please refer to "Recommended Readings for Survivors" in the Appendix. You will find information, practical advice, and comforting words in the books listed there.

After the funeral/memorial service, you will need to locate the will, any life insurance policies, and other pertinent legal and financial information. In some circumstances you will need to design and order a headstone. The following chapters will be most useful.

Chapter II

BRIEF PERSONAL HISTORY

BRIEF PERSONAL HISTORY

The unexamined life is not worth living.

Socrates

Full Name _____

Also Known As _____

Address _____

_____Phone _____

Secondary Address _____

_____Phone _____

Date of Birth _____

Place of Birth _____

Social Security Number _____

Citizenship _____

Marital Status _____

IMMEDIATE FAMILY
NOTE: *If any relatives are deceased, put burial information on address line.*

Parents
Mother (Include maiden name.) _____

Address _____

_____Phone _____

Born_____Died _____

Place of Birth _____

Father _____

Address _____

_____Phone _____

Born_____Died _____

Place of Birth_____

Stepparent _____

Address _____

_____Phone _____

Born_____Died _____

Place of Birth_____

Stepparent _____

Address _____

_____Phone _____

Born_____Died _____

Place of Birth_____

Time, like an ever-rolling stream, Bears all its sons away....

Isaac Watts

Spouse/Partner
If applicable, include wife's maiden name.

Name of Spouse or Partner _____

Address _____

_____Phone _____

Marriage Date _____Place _____

Born_____Died _____

Previous Spouse/Partner
If applicable, include maiden name.

Name of Previous Spouse or Partner _____

Address _____

_____Phone _____

Marriage Date _____Place_____Date of Divorce _____

Born_____Died _____

Name of Previous Spouse or Partner _____

Address _____

_____Phone _____

Marriage Date _____Place_____Date of Divorce _____

Born_____Died _____

Children

Name _____

Address _____

_____Phone _____

Born_____Died _____

Spouse _____

Marriage Date _____Place _____

Name _____

Address _____

_____Phone _____

Born_____Died _____

Spouse _____

Marriage Date _____Place _____

Name _____

Address _____

_____Phone _____

Born_____Died _____

Spouse _____

Marriage Date _____Place _____

Children

Name _____

Address _____

_____Phone _____

Born_____Died _____

Spouse _____

Marriage Date _____Place _____

Name _____

Address _____

_____Phone _____

Born_____Died _____

Spouse _____

Marriage Date _____Place _____

Name _____

Address _____

_____Phone _____

Born_____Died _____

Spouse _____

Marriage Date _____Place _____

Name _____

Address _____

_____Phone _____

Born_____Died _____

Spouse_____

Marriage Date _____Place _____

Name _____

Address _____

_____Phone _____

Born_____Died _____

Spouse_____

Marriage Date _____Place _____

Name _____

Address _____

_____Phone _____

Born_____Died _____

Spouse_____

Marriage Date _____Place _____

Grandchildren

Name _____

Address _____

_____Phone _____

Born_____Died _____

Parents_____

Spouse _____Marriage Date _____

Name _____

Address _____

_____Phone _____

Born_____Died _____

Parents_____

Spouse _____Marriage Date _____

Name _____

Address _____

_____Phone _____

Born_____Died _____

Parent _____

Spouse _____Marriage Date _____

Name _____

Address _____

_____Phone _____

Born_____Died _____

Parents_____

Spouse _____Marriage Date _____

Name _____

Address _____

_____Phone _____

Born_____Died _____

Parents_____

Spouse _____Marriage Date _____

Name _____

Address _____

_____Phone _____

Born_____Died _____

Parents_____

Spouse _____Marriage Date _____

Grandchildren

Name _____

Address _____

_____Phone _____

Born_____Died _____

Parents_____

Spouse _____Marriage Date _____

Name _____

Address _____

_____Phone _____

Born_____Died _____

Parents_____

Spouse _____Marriage Date _____

Name _____

Address _____

_____Phone _____

Born_____Died _____

Parents_____

Spouse _____Marriage Date _____

Name _____

Address _____

_____Phone _____

Born_____Died _____

Parents_____

Spouse _____Marriage Date _____

Name _____

Address _____

_____Phone _____

Born_____Died _____

Parents_____

Spouse _____Marriage Date _____

Name _____

Address _____

_____Phone _____

Born_____Died _____

Parents_____

Spouse _____Marriage Date _____

Grandchildren

Name _____

Address _____

_____Phone _____

Born_____Died _____

Parents_____

Spouse _____Marriage Date _____

Name _____

Address _____

_____Phone _____

Born_____Died _____

Parents_____

Spouse _____Marriage Date _____

Name _____

Address _____

_____Phone _____

Born_____Died _____

Parents_____

Spouse _____Marriage Date _____

Great-Grandchildren

Name _____

Address _____

_____Phone _____

Born_____Died _____

Parents_____

Spouse _____Marriage Date _____

Name _____

Address _____

_____Phone _____

Born_____Died _____

Parents_____

Spouse _____Marriage Date _____

Name _____

Address _____

_____Phone _____

Born_____Died _____

Parents_____

Spouse _____Marriage Date _____

Great-Grandchildren

Name _____

Address _____

_____Phone _____

Born_____Died _____

Parents_____

Spouse _____Marriage Date _____

Name _____

Address _____

_____Phone _____

Born_____Died _____

Parents_____

Spouse _____Marriage Date _____

Name _____

Address _____

_____Phone _____

Born_____Died _____

Parents_____

Spouse _____Marriage Date _____

Brothers and Sisters

Name _____

Address _____

_____Phone _____

Born_____Died _____

Spouse _____

Marriage Date _____Place _____

Name _____

Address _____

_____Phone _____

Born_____Died _____

Spouse _____

Marriage Date _____Place _____

Name _____

Address _____

_____Phone _____

Born_____Died _____

Spouse _____

Marriage Date _____Place _____

Brothers and Sisters

Name _____

Address _____

_____Phone _____

Born_____Died _____

Spouse _____

Marriage Date _____Place _____

Name _____

Address _____

_____Phone _____

Born_____Died _____

Spouse _____

Marriage Date _____Place _____

Name _____

Address _____

_____Phone _____

Born_____Died _____

Spouse _____

Marriage Date _____Place _____

Name _____

Address _____

_____Phone _____

Born_____Died _____

Spouse_____

Marriage Date _____Place _____

Name _____

Address _____

_____Phone _____

Born_____Died _____

Spouse_____

Marriage Date _____Place _____

Name _____

Address _____

_____Phone _____

Born_____Died _____

Spouse_____

Marriage Date _____Place _____

Nieces and Nephews

Name _____

Address _____

_____Phone _____

Born_____Died _____

Parents_____

Spouse _____Marriage Date _____

Name _____

Address _____

_____Phone _____

Born_____Died _____

Parents_____

Spouse _____Marriage Date _____

Name _____

Address _____

_____Phone _____

Born_____Died _____

Parents_____

Spouse _____Marriage Date _____

Name _____

Address _____

_____Phone _____

Born_____Died _____

Parents_____

Spouse _____Marriage Date _____

Name _____

Address _____

_____Phone _____

Born_____Died _____

Parents_____

Spouse _____Marriage Date _____

Name _____

Address _____

_____Phone _____

Born_____Died _____

Parents_____

Spouse _____Marriage Date _____

Nieces and Nephews

Name _____

Address _____

_____ Phone _____

Born_____ Died _____

Parents_____

Spouse _____ Marriage Date _____

Name _____

Address _____

_____ Phone _____

Born_____ Died _____

Parents_____

Spouse _____ Marriage Date _____

Name _____

Address _____

_____ Phone _____

Born_____ Died _____

Parents_____

Spouse _____ Marriage Date _____

EDUCATIONAL HISTORY

Elementary School_____

Address _____

Years _____to _____Year Graduated _____

No man is rich enough to buy back his past.

Oscar Wilde

Elementary School_____

Address _____

Years _____to _____Year Graduated _____

Junior High or Middle School _____

Address _____

Years _____to _____Year Graduated _____

Junior High or Middle School _____

Address _____

Years _____to _____Year Graduated _____

EDUCATIONAL HISTORY

High School _____

Address _____

Years _____to _____Year Graduated _____

Honors/Awards _____

_____

_____

_____

☐ Check if you wish notification of your death to be made. You may wish to include your alumni association in Chapter VI.

High School _____

Address _____

Years _____to _____Year Graduated _____

Honors/Awards _____

_____

_____

_____

☐ Check if you wish notification of your death to be made. You may wish to include your alumni association in Chapter VI.

Vocational/Technical School _____

Address _____

Years _____to _____Year Graduated _____

Honors/Awards _____

_____

_____

_____

☐ Check if you wish notification of your death to be made. You may wish to include your alumni association in Chapter VI.

College _____

Address _____

Years _____to _____Degree_____

Honors/Awards (Academic, student government, clubs, sports, etc.) _____

_____

_____

_____

_____

☐ Check if you wish notification of your death to be made. You may wish to include your alumni association in Chapter VI.

EDUCATIONAL HISTORY

College _____

Address _____

Years _____to _____Degree_____

Honors/Awards (Academic, student government, clubs, sports, etc.) _____

_____

_____

_____

☐ Check if you wish notification of your death to be made. You may wish to include your alumni association in Chapter VI.

University _____

Address _____

Years _____to _____Degree_____

Honors/Awards (Academic, student government, clubs, sports, etc.) _____

_____

_____

_____

☐ Check if you wish notification of your death to be made. You may wish to include your alumni association in Chapter VI.

University _____

Address _____

Years _____to _____Degree_____

Honors/Awards (Academic, student government, clubs, sports, etc.) _____

_____

_____

_____

☐ Check if you wish notification of your death to be made. You may wish to include your alumni association in Chapter VI.

University _____

Address _____

Years _____to _____Degree_____

Honors/Awards (Academic, student government, clubs, sports, etc.) _____

_____

_____

_____

☐ Check if you wish notification of your death to be made. You may wish to include your alumni association in Chapter VI.

EDUCATIONAL HISTORY

If fame is to come only after death, I am in no hurry for it.

Marcus Valerius Martial

University _____

Address _____

Years _____to _____Degree_____

Honors/Awards (Academic, student government, clubs, sports, etc.) _____

_____

_____

_____

☐ Check if you wish notification of your death to be made. You may wish to include your alumni association in Chapter VI.

College Fraternal or Service Organizations

_____

_____

_____

_____

_____

_____

_____

_____

☐ Check if you wish notification of your death to be made.

SERVICE: MILITARY, PEACE CORPS, FOREIGN

Include dates, rank at discharge, branch, assignments, posts, serial number, etc.

_____

_____

_____

_____

_____

_____

_____

_____

_____

_____

_____

FOR VETERANS: *Veterans are eligible for free burial in a military cemetery. You are also entitled to a free headstone or grave marker from the Veterans Affairs Department. Your spouse will need to know the location of your separation/discharge papers. Include this information in Chapter XI.*

FOR SURVIVORS: *Contact your local Veterans Service Office or Veterans Affairs Office for information on the various benefits available. See Chapter XI for the location of separation/discharge papers.*

EMPLOYMENT HISTORY
List in chronological order.

Employer _____

Address _____

_____Phone _____

Years _____through_____Title _____

Type of Employment_____

Contact Person _____

☐ Check if you wish notification of your death to be made.

Employer _____

Address _____

_____Phone _____

Years _____through_____Title _____

Type of Employment_____

Contact Person _____

☐ Check if you wish notification of your death to be made.

Employer _____

Address _____

_____Phone _____

Years _____through_____Title _____

Type of Employment_____

Contact Person _____

☐ Check if you wish notification of your death to be made.

Employer_____

Address _____

_____Phone _____

Years _____through_____Title _____

Type of Employment_____

Contact Person _____

☐ Check if you wish notification of your death to be made.

Employer_____

Address _____

_____Phone _____

Years _____through_____Title _____

Type of Employment_____

Contact Person _____

☐ Check if you wish notification of your death to be made.

Employer_____

Address _____

_____Phone _____

Years _____through_____Title _____

Type of Employment_____

Contact Person _____

☐ Check if you wish notification of your death to be made.

EMPLOYMENT HISTORY

Employer_____

Address _____

_____Phone _____

Years _____through_____Title _____

Type of Employment_____

Contact Person _____

☐ Check if you wish notification of your death to be made.

Employer_____

Address _____

_____Phone _____

Years _____through_____Title _____

Type of Employment_____

Contact Person _____

☐ Check if you wish notification of your death to be made.

Employer_____

Address _____

_____Phone _____

Years _____through_____Title _____

Type of Employment_____

Contact Person _____

☐ Check if you wish notification of your death to be made.

Employer_____

Address _____

_____Phone _____

Years _____through_____Title _____

Type of Employment _____

Contact Person _____

☐ Check if you wish notification of your death to be made.

Employer_____

Address _____

_____Phone _____

Years _____through_____Title _____

Type of Employment _____

Contact Person _____

☐ Check if you wish notification of your death to be made.

Employer_____

Address _____

_____Phone _____

Years _____through_____Title _____

Type of Employment _____

Contact Person _____

☐ Check if you wish notification of your death to be made.

HONORS, AWARDS, ACCOMPLISHMENTS, TRAINING

List those not included elsewhere. These could include community, state, national, or work-related honors. Include dates.

_____

_____

_____

_____

_____

_____

_____

_____

_____

_____

_____

_____

_____

_____

Chapter III

OTHER FAMILY MEMBERS
TO BE NOTIFIED

OTHER FAMILY MEMBERS TO BE NOTIFIED

(List any additional family members not listed in Chapter II.)

Nature's law, that man was made to mourn.

Robert Burns

Name _____

Relationship _____

Address _____

_____Phone _____

Name _____

Relationship _____

Address _____

_____Phone _____

Name _____

Relationship _____

Address _____

_____Phone _____

Name _____

Relationship _____

Address _____

_____Phone _____

Name _____

Relationship _____

Address _____

_____Phone _____

Name _____

Relationship _____

Address _____

_____Phone _____

Name _____

Relationship _____

Address _____

_____Phone _____

Name _____

Relationship _____

Address _____

_____Phone _____

Name _____

Relationship _____

Address _____

_____Phone _____

Name _____

Relationship _____

Address _____

_____Phone _____

Name _____

Relationship _____

Address _____

_____Phone _____

Name _____

Relationship _____

Address _____

_____Phone _____

Name _____

Relationship _____

Address _____

_____Phone _____

Name _____

Relationship _____

Address _____

_____Phone _____

Name _____

Relationship _____

Address _____

_____Phone _____

Name _____

Relationship _____

Address _____

_____Phone _____

OTHER FAMILY MEMBERS TO BE NOTIFIED

Name _____

Relationship _____

Address _____

_____Phone _____

Name _____

Relationship _____

Address _____

_____Phone _____

Name _____

Relationship _____

Address _____

_____Phone _____

Name _____

Relationship _____

Address _____

_____Phone _____

Chapter

IV

FRIENDS TO BE NOTIFIED

FRIENDS TO BE NOTIFIED

If your address book is up-to-date and should be used, note its location here:_____

Mailing a printed memorial card or a memorial service program is often the easiest method for survivors to notify your out-of-town friends. These are available from the funeral home or you may design your own. See section on memorial service program in Chapter VIII.

Name _____

Address _____

_____Phone _____

Name _____

Address _____

_____Phone _____

Name _____

Address _____

_____Phone _____

Name _____

Address _____

_____Phone _____

Name _____

Address _____

_____Phone _____

Name _____

Address _____

_____Phone _____

Name _____

Address _____

_____Phone _____

Name _____

Address _____

_____Phone _____

Name _____

Address _____

_____Phone _____

To lose a friend is the greatest of all losses.

Publius Syrus

Name _____

Address _____

_____Phone _____

Name _____

Address _____

_____Phone _____

Name _____

Address _____

_____Phone _____

Name _____

Address _____

_____Phone _____

Name _____

Address _____

_____Phone _____

Name _____

Address _____

_____Phone _____

Name _____

Address _____

_____Phone _____

Name _____

Address _____

_____Phone _____

Name _____

Address _____

_____Phone _____

Name _____

Address _____

_____Phone _____

 FRIENDS TO BE NOTIFIED

Name _____

Address _____

_____Phone _____

Name _____

Address _____

_____Phone _____

Name _____

Address _____

_____Phone _____

Name _____

Address _____

_____Phone _____

Name _____

Address _____

_____Phone _____

Chapter

V

EMPLOYEES/CO-WORKERS TO BE NOTIFIED

Employees/Co-workers To Be Notified

Name _____

Address _____

_____Phone _____

Name _____

Address _____

_____Phone _____

Name _____

Address _____

_____Phone _____

Name _____

Address _____

_____Phone _____

Name _____

Address _____

_____Phone _____

EMPLOYEES/CO-WORKERS TO BE NOTIFIED

EMPLOYEES/CO-WORKERS TO BE NOTIFIED

Name _____

Address _____

_____Phone _____

Name _____

Address _____

_____Phone _____

Name _____

Address _____

_____Phone _____

Name _____

Address _____

_____Phone _____

Name _____

Address _____

_____Phone _____

Chapter

VI

ORGANIZATIONS TO CONTACT

ORGANIZATIONS TO CONTACT

PLACES OF WORSHIP

Name _____

Address _____

_____Phone _____

Contact Person _____

Name _____

Address _____

_____Phone _____

Contact Person _____

RELIGIOUS ORGANIZATIONS

Name _____

Address _____

_____Phone _____

Contact Person _____

Name _____

Address _____

_____Phone _____

Contact Person _____

CLUBS

Club _____

Address _____

_____Phone _____

Contact Person _____

Club _____

Address _____

_____Phone _____

Contact Person _____

Club _____

Address _____

_____Phone _____

Contact Person _____

Club _____

Address _____

_____Phone _____

Contact Person _____

Life's too short for chess.

H. J. Byron

ASSOCIATIONS

One approaches the journey's end. But the end is a goal, not a catastrophe.

George Sand

Association _____

Address _____

_____Phone _____

Contact Person _____

Association _____

Address _____

_____Phone _____

Contact Person _____

Association _____

Address _____

_____Phone _____

Contact Person _____

Association _____

Address _____

_____Phone _____

Contact Person _____

Chapter
VII

OBITUARY

OBITUARY INFORMATION

Obituaries usually include personal statistics and family information listed in Chapter II. You may choose to write your own detailed obituary summarizing this information and including other important facts. Or, you may simply refer the reader to the earlier sections and note here any information you would particularly like to have published.

Some newspapers use a standard format for obituaries and provide a form which, when completed, contains all the necessary information. An obituary may also be used to announce the date and time of a memorial service. Death notices merely stating that an individual has died are generally published at no charge. Funeral notices are paid advertisements bought by the family of the deceased. They include information not normally included in obituaries and may include a photo. Before you write your obituary, check with your local newspaper to learn their rates. Lengthy obituaries can be expensive. See the Appendix for obituary examples, or read the obituary page in your local newspaper.

What I Would Like Included In My Obituary
You may wish to write your obituary or funeral notice in this space. If there is a photo that you would like used, attach it at the end of the chapter or place it in the envelope at the back of this book.

_____

_____

_____

_____

_____

_____

Attach Your Photo Here

Chapter VIII

FUNERAL AND MEMORIAL

FUNERAL AND MEMORIAL SERVICE

NOTE: *Please read the entire chapter before making decisions.*

When you plan for your funeral and/or memorial service and the disposition of your remains, take into consideration both your wishes and the values of whoever will be responsible for carrying out your decisions. Some of your ideas may fly in the face of family customs or religious beliefs; consider the likely emotional responses of family and friends to any nontraditional or unusual plans that you may make. You may wish to discuss the rationale for your decisions or put it in writing in this book. Most people will want the rituals following death to provide comfort and closure for the survivors. Please note that the choices you document in *Last Wishes* are not legally binding. By discussing any nontraditional plans with those who will be charged with their fulfillment, you can help overcome resistance and ensure smoother implementation of your choices at the time of your death.

You may want to have a traditional funeral service where hymns are sung, a religious personage talks about you, and your body is present. However, there are many other possibilities. In an unplanned service there is often a universal "fill in the blanks" speech given about the deceased. *Last Wishes* provides an opportunity to make the funeral or memorial service more personal—to include what you would like to be mentioned. You may have favorite poetry you would like read or music to be played. This chapter gives you an opportunity to note these choices.

Some people want a simple cremation with no service. If this is your choice, discuss it with family or friends in addition to recording your plans. The person charged with carrying out your plans may feel that others will be critical and won't understand. There are some people for whom the absence of a service might denote a lack of love or respect for the deceased. Having your preferences in writing and discussing them in advance will offer your survivors some protection from such criticism.

There are various options available when you plan for the disposal of your remains. Burial in a casket is a common choice, but more and more people are choosing cremation; the ashes that remain (the "cremains") can be buried, kept in an urn, or scattered (depending on local regulations). Another option is entombment in a mausoleum. Or, you may wish to donate your body to a medical school. Some funeral homes and crematories also offer a less expensive "direct disposition" option, often advertised as "direct burial" or "direct cremation." The body is taken from the place of death directly to the cemetery or crematory, eliminating intermediate services such as preparation, storage of body, and visitation.

Caskets vary widely in price, style, and type. If burial in a casket is your choice, indicate the type of casket you wish and the approximate price range in the space on page 84. Choosing a casket without any guidelines is a very emotional decision for survivors and they may feel that they should select a more expensive model than you would wish. If you desire to have a "simple pine box," it is best to locate or build one and have it set aside until needed (see "Unusual Funeral or Burial Ideas" in the Appendix).

If you should choose cremation, there are also several alternatives. Cremation is generally the least expensive option, aside from donating one's body to a medical school. Keep in mind, however, that some survivors strongly desire to view the body of the deceased one final time. It may be possible to have the body displayed in a rental casket for the service and then cremated afterwards.

You may wish to select a funeral home and cemetery in order to make all arrangements in advance. If so, make an appointment to interview the director and to inspect each facility you are considering. Ask for a copy of their price list for all services and costs (e.g., casket, various professional services, limousine, other vehicles, musicians, honoraria, cemetery plot, vault, grave liner, etc.). The information you gather will help you make the necessary decisions regarding the disposition of your remains.

Ask funeral directors about their willingness to adhere to your wishes as expressed in this book. At each cemetery, request a list of restrictions. What kind of flowers and markers are permitted? Is a grave liner or vault required? Ask if there is security against vandalism and if there are trust documents to assure perpetual care of the cemetery.

In choosing among these alternatives, think of the cost and also

Funeral pomp is more for the vanity of the living than for the honor of the dead.

François, Duc de La Rochefoucauld

anticipate the reactions of your family or friends as you complete the following sections. Please read the entire chapter through before making any decisions.

VETERANS NOTE: *You may be eligible for burial in a military cemetery at no charge. In some cases spouses and minor children may also be eligible. Contact your local Veterans Administration Office for more information.*

FUNERAL ARRANGEMENTS

Check or initial where appropriate to indicate your preference. You may wish to write "no" in some blanks to make your wishes even clearer.

☐ I am a member of a Memorial Society.

Society _____

Address _____

_____Phone _____

Contact Person _____

Location of Documents _____

☐ I am the owner of a Pre-need Plan.

Name of Plan _____

Address _____

_____Phone _____

Contact Person _____

Location of Documents _____

☐ I have pre-paid for Direct Disposition.

Name of Plan _____

Address _____

_____Phone _____

Contact Person _____

Location of Documents _____

Preferred Funeral Home or Crematory

Name _____

Address _____

_____Phone _____

Contact Person _____

Alternative Funeral Home or Crematory

If you have a secondary residence, you may want to list an alternate funeral home or crematory.

Name _____

Address _____

_____Phone _____

Contact Person _____

☐ If I die at an out-of-state location, I wish for my remains to be transported to one of the above.

☐ If I die at an out-of-state location, do not transport my remains. Make funeral arrangements where I die.

☐ I wish an autopsy (postmortem) to be performed. (This procedure may be required in certain situations.)

☐ I do not wish to have an autopsy performed unless required by law.

☐ I wish for my remains to be embalmed. (This procedure may be required in some jurisdictions in certain situations.)

☐ I do not wish to be embalmed unless it is required by law.

☐ No preference. To be determined by _____

Type of Funeral and/or Memorial Service

☐ Non-religious service

☐ Religious service

☐ Private service

☐ Graveside service

☐ Public service

☐ Casket/Urn present during service

☐ Service to follow burial/cremation

☐ Service to precede burial/cremation

☐ No service. Dispose of remains immediately. See Chapter IX.

☐ No preference. To be determined by _____

Would Like Service to be Held at

Facility _____

Address _____

_____Phone _____

Would Like to Preside

Name _____

Address _____

_____Phone _____

Would Like a Eulogy Given By

Name _____

Address _____

_____Phone _____

The web of our life is of a mingled yarn, Good and ill together.

Shakespeare

Suggest some things that you would like mentioned about you during the service.

_____

_____

_____

_____

_____

_____

_____

_____

_____

_____

_____

_____

_____

Death never takes the wise man by surprise, He is always ready to go.

Jean de La Fontaine

Favorite Hymn or Other Music to Be Played

Specify soloist or group requested to perform, if any.

_____

_____

_____

_____

_____

_____

_____

_____

Recorded Music to Be Played

It would be helpful to have already taped your choices of music. Designate the location of tapes, records, or CDs in this section.

_____

_____

_____

_____

_____

_____

Favorite Poem or Other Reading to Be Included in Service
Attach copies or designate location.

_____

_____

_____

_____

_____

_____

_____

_____

_____

_____

_____

_____

_____

_____

_____

Funeral/Memorial Service Program

You may wish to design a program or card for your funeral/memorial service. Indicate the order of the ceremony and any text or poetry to be included. If there is a photo that you would like reproduced on the cover, attach it here or place it in the envelope at the back of this book.

_____

_____

_____

_____

_____

_____

_____

_____

_____

_____

_____

_____

_____

_____

_____

_____

_____

_____

_____

_____

_____

_____

_____

_____

_____

_____

_____

_____

_____

_____

_____

_____

_____

_____

_____

_____

_____

_____

_____

_____

_____

_____

_____

_____

_____

_____

_____

_____

_____

_____

_____

_____

PALLBEARERS

Usually six to eight active pallbearers are chosen to lift and carry the casket. Some may be honorary pallbearers if they are not able to lift casket.

Active Pallbearers

Name _____ Phone _____

Name _____ Phone _____

Name _____ Phone _____

Name _____ Phone _____

Name _____ Phone _____

Name _____ Phone _____

Name _____ Phone _____

Name _____ Phone _____

Honorary Pallbearers

You may choose as many honorary pallbearers as you wish. This is a way to honor persons who were very important to you and have them mentioned.

Name _____ Phone _____

Name _____ Phone _____

Name _____ Phone _____

Name _____ Phone _____

Name _____ Phone _____

Name _____ Phone _____

Honorary Pallbearers

Name _____ Phone _____

Name _____ Phone _____

Name _____ Phone _____

Name _____ Phone _____

FUNERAL PROCESSION

My preferred procession route from the funeral home to the cemetery, if any, follows. For example, the route may include passing your home, childhood home, place of business, etc. Consider the expense involved in funeral staff time, vehicle rental, and police escort. If there is to be no procession, note that here.

_____

_____

_____

_____

_____

_____

_____

_____

_____

_____

ADDITIONAL PREFERENCES

List any unique and creative ideas that may not be standard funeral practice; for example, choose a photograph or portrait to be on display, specify the location of a wake and choose the food and drink to be served, etc. Some services include a "video tribute" to the deceased. You may want to create your own videotape of what you consider to be the highlights of your life. If you are concerned about the length of your funeral or memorial service, you may wish to set some time limits here. For more suggestions, see "Unusual Funeral or Burial Ideas" in the Appendix.

The following are my special wishes regarding the type of service I desire:

_____

_____

_____

_____

_____

_____

_____

_____

_____

_____

FUNERAL AND MEMORIAL SERVICE

_____

_____

_____

_____

_____

_____

_____

_____

_____

_____

_____

_____

_____

_____

_____

_____

_____

_____

_____

CASKET AND VIEWING PREFERENCES

☐ Open casket

☐ Closed casket

☐ Casket to be open only at the following times _____

☐ Casket to be draped with flag (specify country or organization)_____

_____

☐ Purchase casket. Type and price range of casket_____

_____

☐ Rental casket for service (to be followed by cremation)

☐ No casket: cremate remains immediately

☐ No preference. To be determined by _____

I Would Like to Wear the Following Clothing
Designate the location of any item that might be difficult to find.

_____

_____

_____

_____

_____

_____

_____

_____

I Would Like to Wear the Following Jewelry

Designate the location of any item that might be difficult to find and note whether or not the jewelry should be removed prior to the final disposition of the body.

_____

_____

_____

_____

_____

_____

_____

I Would Like the Following Additional Items to Be Placed in the Casket with Me

For example, you might list a favorite book, photo, golf club, tennis racket, bottle of wine, flag, flowers, etc. Designate the location of any item that might be difficult to find. Funeral directors often discourage burying jewelry or items of great value.

_____

_____

_____

_____

_____

_____

FLOWER PREFERENCES

Specify type and arrangements. Note that certain types of flowers may be out of season and very costly to obtain. It may be wise to give alternate choices.

_____

_____

_____

_____

_____

_____

MEMORIAL DONATION

In lieu of flowers, I request that a memorial donation be sent to the following organization(s):

Organization _____

_____

Address _____

_____Phone _____

Contact Person _____

Purpose of Donation _____

☐ Whatever the organization designates as its greatest need

Organization _____

Address _____

_____ Phone _____

Contact Person _____

Purpose of Donation _____

☐ Whatever the organization designates as its greatest need

Each person is born to one posses- sion which outlives all his others—his last breath.

Mark Twain

Organization _____

Address _____

_____ Phone _____

Contact Person _____

Purpose of Donation _____

☐ Whatever the organization designates as its greatest need

Organization _____

Address _____

_____ Phone _____

Contact Person _____

Purpose of Donation _____

☐ Whatever the organization designates as its greatest need

A MEMORIAL TO BE DESIGNATED

Some possibilities include establishing a special trust fund, scholarship fund, speakers' fund, award or prize, tree planting, park bench, plaque, or other lasting memorial.

_____

_____

_____

_____

_____

_____

INSCRIPTION

If a building, room, scholarship, speakers' fund, tree planting, etc., were to be dedicated to your memory, what inscription would you like on the memorial?

_____

_____

_____

_____

_____

_____

_____

_____

So little done, so much to do.
Cecil Rhodes

Chapter
IX

DISPOSITION OF REMAINS

DISPOSITION OF REMAINS

Check or initial where appropriate to indicate your preference. You may wish to write "no" in some blanks to make your wishes even clearer. NOTE: *Please read the entire chapter before making decisions.*

DONATION OF BODY

List any special arrangements. Attach forms if available. See information regarding the Living Bank listed under "Organizations" in the Appendix.

Write "No" if a donation is not authorized: _____

☐ Donation of Body to Medical or Dental School

Note that some medical schools require that the donor or survivors make arrangements with, and pay for, a funeral director to do a preliminary embalming of the body and to transport the body to the facility. Most State Anatomical Boards cannot accept a body for donation under certain conditions. These conditions may include prior autopsy, death caused by a crushing injury, death caused by a highly contagious disease, and a body with broken bones, recent surgery, or external cancer. Contact your State Anatomical Board or a medical school for more information. In Florida, for example, after the body has been studied, the Anatomical Board pays to have the body cremated. The ashes can then be returned to the next of kin, placed in a cemetery, or scattered over the Gulf of Mexico.

Arrangements: _____

_____

_____

_____

_____

DONATION OF ORGANS

Organ banks often prefer donations from those who are without contagious disease and who are under the age of forty. An exception may be corneas used by eye banks. However, according to the Living Bank in Houston, the organ procurement team evaluates the condition of all usable organs at the time of the donor's death. Every medically acceptable organ is used. Donated tissue can be used despite advancing age. The recipients of the organs pay all of the costs. There is no cost to the donor.

Write "No" if a donation is not authorized: _____

☐ Donation of organs as specified below

ORGAN   ORGANIZATION

_____   _____

_____   _____

_____   _____

_____   _____

_____   _____

_____   _____

_____   _____

_____   _____

CREMATION OPTIONS

☐ Cremation of remains

☐ Cremate in casket

☐ Cremate in least expensive manner allowed by state law

☐ Urn burial at _____

NOTE: *If burial is to be at a cemetery, there will be a charge for opening and closing the grave.*

☐ Urn in niche at _____

☐ Ashes to be scattered as follows

NOTE: *There may be local restrictions as to where ashes can be scattered.*

_____

_____

_____

_____

_____

_____

_____

_____

_____

Why is it we rejoice at a birth and grieve at a funeral? It is because we are not the person involved.

Mark Twain

BURIAL OPTIONS

☐ Burial without cremation

☐ Private burial/committal

☐ Public burial/committal

☐ No preference. To be determined by _____

VETERANS NOTE: *You may be eligible for burial in a military cemetery at no charge. In some cases spouses and minor children may also be eligible. Contact your local Veterans Administration Office for more information.*

☐ I wish to be entombed in a mausoleum at

Cemetery_____

Address_____Phone _____

Contact Person _____

Mausoleum space has been purchased   ☐ YES   ☐ NO

Location of mausoleum deed _____

☐ I wish to be buried in a cemetery plot at

Cemetery_____

Address _____

Address_____Phone _____

Contact Person _____

Cemetery plot has been purchased   ☐ YES   ☐ NO

Location of cemetery plot ownership papers _____

VAULT ENCLOSURES

NOTE: *Sometimes a grave liner or vault is required by a cemetery to help prevent sunken graves. Note your preference here.*

☐ I prefer a grave liner

☐ I prefer a vault

☐ If not required, I do not want either

SPECIAL BURIAL INSTRUCTIONS

My friends should drink a dozen of Claret on my tomb.

John Keats

_____

_____

_____

_____

_____

_____

_____

_____

_____

_____

_____

Chapter X

DESIGN YOUR OWN HEADSTONE

DESIGN YOUR OWN HEADSTONE

It is a far, far better rest that I go to, than I have ever known.

Charles Dickens

There may be cemetery restrictions as to the type allowed. Some cemeteries allow only flat markers to make lawn maintenance easier. Memorials are usually made of granite, marble, or bronze. You may wish to visit a monument company and look at different types of markers and headstones to compare styles and costs. If funds are limited, consider whether you wish to emphasize the above-ground memorial or the coffin and grave liner which will be buried and never seen again. If you don't specify your wishes, it is likely that your grave marker will simply list your name, year of birth, and year of death.

Price Range for Headstone or Marker

_____

Desired Inscription

_____

_____

_____

_____

_____

_____

Design Your Headstone in This Space

Chapter

XI

LEGAL AND INSURANCE INFORMATION

LEGAL AND INSURANCE INFORMATION

NOTE: *This section is not intended to take the place of formal legal documents. Please consult with your attorney as you organize your estate.*

LEGAL INFORMATION

What you leave at your death, let it be without controversy, else the lawyers will be your heirs.

Sir Thomas Browne

Attorney _____

Address _____

_____

Office Phone _____Home Phone_____

Power of Attorney

The term "Power of Attorney" generally means that you have conferred upon another person the legally recognized authority to perform certain acts on your behalf. A standard Power of Attorney is terminated in the event that you become incapacitated. However, more than 40 states have passed laws allowing for a "Durable Power of Attorney for Health Care." This means that you may legally appoint someone to act on your behalf to make decisions concerning your medical treatment, including your right to refuse medical treatment.

The conditions under which you would not want medical treatment are written in a Living Will or Advance Directive. Please seek legal advice regarding creating a Durable Power of Attorney and/or a Living Will. Please note that either of these may be revoked by you at any time.

All hospitals, nursing homes, hospice programs, and home health care agencies that receive Medicare and Medicaid funding are required by the Patient Self-Determination Act to give all adult patients information on "advance directives." An Advance Directive is a written instruction on the type of health care that should be provided when and if the individual is incapacitated. An Advance Directive can be a Durable Power of Attorney for Health Care, a Living Will, instructions regarding designating a health care surrogate, or instructions about a terminally ill person's right to refuse medical treatment to prolong his or her life by artificial means. Each agency must document whether the patient has an advance directive, the discussion with the patient regarding an advance directive, and the patient's response. This law does not require that you have an advance directive; it is meant to provide the adult patient with the information and the opportunity to make an advance decision.

Power of Attorney

Name _____

Address _____

_____

Office Phone _____Home Phone _____

Document Location _____

Type _____

Time Period_____

Durable Power of Attorney for Health Care

Name _____

Address _____

_____

Office Phone _____Home Phone _____

Document Location _____

Time Period_____

Living Will

This varies from state to state, but generally expresses your wishes regarding the use of life-sustaining procedures in the event of a terminal condition. If you live in more than one state during the year, it may be advisable to have a correct living will for each state. Please seek legal advice. A copy of a Florida Living Will is contained in the Appendix as an example. Contact Choice In Dying (listed under "Organizations" in the Appendix) for a free Advance Directive packet that complies with your state's law.

Also, you can get a copy of the "Medical Directive," which can be used as a Living Will, from Harvard Medical School by sending a self-addressed, stamped, business-size #10 envelope to HMS Health Publications Group, Dept. MD, P.O. Box 380, Boston, MA 02117. The cost: two copies for $5.00 (put 55¢ postage on return envelope) or five copies for $10.00 (put 78¢ postage on return envelope). Make checks payable to Harvard Medical School.

Location of Living Will _____

_____

_____

NOTE: *It is recommended that you give signed copies of your Living Will to your relatives, attorney, and physician(s) and that you keep a copy in a bank safety deposit box. If you are in a nursing home or a hospital, request that your Living Will be made part of your medical record.*

Will

Location of Will _____

Executor _____

Address _____

_____

Office Phone _____ Home Phone _____

Safety Deposit Box

Safety Deposit Box Location _____

Number(s) of Safety Deposit Box(es) _____

Location of Safety Deposit Box Key(s) _____

_____

Others with Access to Box and Key _____

_____

Post Office Box

Number _____

Location _____

Location of Key _____

Important Documents

Location of Birth Certificate _____

_____

Location of Marriage and/or Divorce Certificates _____

_____

Location of Military Service Discharge Papers (if any) _____

_____

Location of Keys, Safe and Lock
Combinations, Computer Passwords, Etc.

_____

_____

_____

_____

_____

_____

_____

Location of Other Important Records
For example, naturalization papers, deeds, titles to property, professional records, death certificates of relatives, religious documents, etc.

_____

_____

_____

_____

_____

_____

_____

INSURANCE

NOTE: *The value of insurance policies and the names of beneficiaries may change. Please review this section from time to time and revise as necessary.*

Life, Accident, and Disability Policies

Policy Type _____

Policy Number _____Value _____

Company _____

Address _____

_____Phone _____

Agent _____Phone _____

Beneficiary(ies) _____

Location of Document _____

Policy Type _____

Policy Number _____Value _____

Company _____

Address _____

_____Phone _____

Agent _____Phone _____

Beneficiary(ies) _____

Location of Document _____

Life, Accident, and Disability Policies

Policy Type _____

Policy Number _____ Value _____

Company _____

Address _____

_____ Phone _____

Agent _____ Phone _____

Beneficiary(ies) _____

Location of Document _____

Policy Type _____

Policy Number _____ Value _____

Company _____

Address _____

_____ Phone _____

Agent _____ Phone _____

Beneficiary(ies) _____

Location of Document _____

Be sure to send a lazy man for the angel of death.

Jewish Proverb

Other Insurance Policies

Auto, Boat, Health, Personal Property, Liability, etc.

NOTE: *Some insurance policies may have a death benefit and beneficiaries.*

Policy Type _____

Policy Number _____

Value of Death Benefit _____

Company _____

Address _____

_____Phone _____

Agent _____Phone _____

Beneficiary(ies) _____

Location of Document _____

Policy Type _____

Policy Number _____

Value of Death Benefit _____

Company _____

Address _____

_____Phone _____

Agent _____Phone _____

Beneficiary(ies) _____

Location of Document _____

LEGAL AND INSURANCE INFORMATION

Policy Type _____

Policy Number _____

Value of Death Benefit _____

Company _____

Address _____

_____Phone _____

Agent _____Phone _____

Beneficiary(ies) _____

Location of Document _____

Other Death Benefits to Which Entitled

_____

_____

_____

_____

_____

_____

_____

_____

_– 108 –_

Chapter XII

ACCOUNTS AND MAJOR ASSETS

ACCOUNTS AND MAJOR ASSETS

NOTE: *This chapter may need to be updated frequently as sources of income, investments, assets, and debts change.*

CHECKING ACCOUNTS

Bank _____

Address _____

_____Phone _____

Account Number_____

Location of Book_____

Bank _____

Address _____

_____Phone _____

Account Number_____

Location of Book_____

Bank _____

Address _____

_____Phone _____

Account Number_____

Location of Book_____

SAVINGS ACCOUNTS

Bank _____

Address _____

_____Phone _____

Account Number_____

Location of Book_____

Bank _____

_____

Address _____

_____Phone _____

Account Number_____

Location of Book_____

Bank _____

Address _____

_____Phone _____

Account Number_____

Location of Book_____

CERTIFICATES OF DEPOSIT

Bank _____

Address _____

_____Phone _____

Account Number_____

Location of Certificate_____

Bank _____

Address _____

_____Phone _____

Account Number_____

Location of Certificate_____

Bank _____

Address _____

_____

_____Phone _____

Account Number_____

Location of Certificate_____

INVESTMENT / BROKERAGE ACCOUNTS

Institution _____

Address _____

_____Phone _____

Broker's Name _____

Account Number_____

Location of Documents _____

Institution _____

Address _____

_____Phone _____

Broker's Name _____

Account Number_____

Location of Documents _____

Institution _____

Address _____

_____Phone _____

Broker's Name _____

Account Number_____

Location of Documents _____

OTHER ACCOUNTS

Type _____

Institution _____

Address _____

_____Phone _____

Contact Person _____

Account Number_____

Location of Documents _____

Type _____

Institution _____

Address _____

_____Phone _____

Contact Person _____

Account Number_____

Location of Documents _____

Location of Records of Stocks, Bonds, Mutual Funds _____

_____

_____

_____

OTHER SOURCES OF INCOME

List the location of documentation and other pertinent information for additional sources of income.

Social Security _____

Pension _____

Pension _____

IRAs, Keoghs, 401(k), etc. _____

IRAs, Keoghs, 401(k), etc. _____

IRAs, Keoghs, 401(k), etc. _____

IRAs, Keoghs, 401(k), etc. _____

IRAs, Keoghs, 401(k), etc. _____

Veterans Benefits _____

Civil Service Benefits _____

Copyright(s) _____

Patent(s) _____

Trust Fund(s)_____

Disability Benefit(s)_____

Other _____

_____

_____

_____

_____

DETAILS OF MAJOR BUSINESS HOLDINGS

_____

_____

_____

_____

_____

_____

_____

Address of Land or Building Owned _____

_____

Address of Land or Building Owned _____

_____

Address of Land or Building Owned _____

_____

List Car(s) Owned and Location of Title(s) _____

_____

_____

_____

_____

List Other Vehicle(s) Owned and Location of Title(s) (Boats, airplanes, motorcy-cles, etc.) _____

_____

_____

_____

_____

ADDITIONAL LAWYERS AND ACCOUNTANTS INVOLVED IN YOUR BUSINESS

Name _____

Title or Position_____

Address _____

_____

Office Phone _____ Home Phone _____

Name _____

Title or Position_____

Address _____

_____

Office Phone _____ Home Phone _____

ADDITIONAL LAWYERS AND ACCOUNTANTS INVOLVED IN YOUR BUSINESS

Name _____

Title or Position_____

Address _____

_____

Office Phone _____Home Phone _____

Name _____

Title or Position_____

Address _____

_____

Office Phone _____Home Phone _____

DEBTS OWED TO ME

Debtor_____

Address _____

_____

Office Phone _____Home Phone _____

Description _____

Terms _____

Balance _____

Location of Documents_____

Debtor _____

Address _____

_____

Office Phone _____Home Phone _____

Description _____

Terms _____

Balance _____

Location of Documents _____

D E B T S   I   O W E

Mortgage Company_____

Address _____

_____Phone _____

Contact Person _____

Terms _____

Balance _____

Location of Documents _____

Account Number_____

Location of Mortgaged Property _____

DEBTS I OWE

Mortgage Company _____

Address _____

_____Phone _____

Contact Person _____

Terms _____

Balance _____

Location of Documents _____

Account Number _____

Location of Mortgaged Property _____

Car Loan Company _____

Address _____

_____Phone _____

Contact Person _____

Terms _____

Balance _____

Location of Documents _____

Account Number _____

Make, Model, and Year of Car _____

Car Loan Company _____

Address _____

_____Phone _____

Contact Person _____

Terms _____

Balance _____

Location of Documents _____

Account Number _____

Make, Model, and Year of Car _____

Other Lender _____

Address _____

_____Phone _____

Contact Person _____

Terms _____

Balance _____

Location of Documents _____

Account Number _____

Description of Property _____

CREDIT CARDS

Card _____

Account Number_____

Company or Bank _____

Address _____

_____Phone _____

☐ Check here if card balance is covered by death benefit

Card _____

Account Number_____

Company or Bank _____

Address _____

_____Phone _____

☐ Check here if card balance is covered by death benefit

Card _____

Account Number_____

Company or Bank _____

Address _____

_____Phone _____

☐ Check here if card balance is covered by death benefit

Card _____

Account Number_____

Company or Bank _____

Address _____

_____Phone _____

☐ Check here if card balance is covered by death benefit

Card _____

Account Number_____

Company or Bank _____

Address _____

_____Phone _____

☐ Check here if card balance is covered by death benefit

Card _____

Account Number_____

Company or Bank _____

Address _____

_____Phone _____

☐ Check here if card balance is covered by death benefit

CREDIT CARDS

There is no wealth but life.

John Ruskin

Card _____

Account Number_____

Company or Bank _____

Address _____

_____Phone _____

☐ Check here if card balance is covered by death benefit

Card _____

Account Number_____

Company or Bank _____

Address _____

_____Phone _____

☐ Check here if card balance is covered by death benefit

Card _____

Account Number_____

Company or Bank _____

Address _____

_____Phone _____

☐ Check here if card balance is covered by death benefit

OTHER FINANCIAL INFORMATION

Income Tax Returns

Preparer _____

Address _____

_____Phone _____

Location of Returns _____

Location of Inventory of Household Contents

_____

_____

_____

_____

A man's real possession is his memory. In nothing else is he rich, in nothing else is he poor.

Alexander Smith

Location of Inventory of Other Personal Property

_____

_____

_____

_____

_____

FREQUENT FLYER MILES

Some airlines may allow you to bequeath frequent flyer miles to your spouse or, in some cases, to another close relative. Check with the airlines you use regarding their policies and, if applicable, clearly spell out your wishes regarding this matter in your will.

Airline _____

Account Number _____

Airline _____

Account Number _____

Airline _____

Account Number _____

Airline _____

Account Number _____

Airline _____

Account Number _____

Airline _____

Account Number _____

Chapter XIII

DISTRIBUTION OF PERSONAL PROPERTY

DISTRIBUTION OF PERSONAL PROPERTY

WISHES REGARDING PERSONAL PROPERTY

NOTE: *This issue should be handled in the will; however, small personal items can be listed here to show your intentions. You may wish to enclose photographs to help to identify certain items.*

All my possessions for a moment of time.

Elizabeth I Queen
of England
(Alleged last words)

Item _____ Leave to _____

Item _____ Leave to _____

Item _____ Leave to _____

Item _____ Leave to _____

Item _____ Leave to _____

Item _____ Leave to _____

Item _____ Leave to _____

Item _____ Leave to _____

Item _____ Leave to _____

Item _____ Leave to _____

Item _____ Leave to _____

Item _____ Leave to _____

Item _____ Leave to _____

Item _____ Leave to _____

Item _____ Leave to _____

Item _____ Leave to _____

Item _____ Leave to _____

Item _____ Leave to _____

Item _____ Leave to _____

Item _____ Leave to _____

Item _____ Leave to _____

Item _____ Leave to _____

Item _____ Leave to _____

Item _____ Leave to _____

Item _____ Leave to _____

Item _____ Leave to _____

Item _____ Leave to _____

Item _____ Leave to _____

Item _____ Leave to _____

Item _____ Leave to _____

Item _____ Leave to _____

Item _____ Leave to _____

Item _____ Leave to _____

Item _____ Leave to _____

Item _____ Leave to _____

Item _____ Leave to _____

Item _____ Leave to _____

Item _____ Leave to _____

Item _____ Leave to _____

Item _____ Leave to _____

Item _____ Leave to _____

Item _____ Leave to _____

Item _____ Leave to _____

Item _____ Leave to _____

Item _____ Leave to _____

Item _____ Leave to _____

Item _____ Leave to _____

Item _____ Leave to _____

Item _____ Leave to _____

Item _____ Leave to _____

Item _____ Leave to _____

Item _____ Leave to _____

Item _____ Leave to _____

Item _____ Leave to _____

Item _____ Leave to _____

Item _____ Leave to _____

Item _____ Leave to _____

Item _____ Leave to _____

Item _____ Leave to _____

Item _____ Leave to _____

Item _____ Leave to _____

Item _____ Leave to _____

Item _____ Leave to _____

Item _____ Leave to _____

Item _____ Leave to _____

Item _____ Leave to _____

Item _____ Leave to _____

Item _____ Leave to _____

Item _____ Leave to _____

Item _____ Leave to _____

Item _____ Leave to _____

Item _____ Leave to _____

Item _____ Leave to _____

Item _____ Leave to _____

Item _____ Leave to _____

Item _____ Leave to _____

Item _____ Leave to _____

Item _____ Leave to _____

Item _____ Leave to _____

Item _____ Leave to _____

Item _____ Leave to _____

Item _____ Leave to _____

Item _____ Leave to _____

Item _____ Leave to _____

Item _____ Leave to _____

Item _____ Leave to _____

Item _____ Leave to _____

Item _____ Leave to _____

Item _____ Leave to _____

Item _____ Leave to _____

Item _____ Leave to _____

Item _____ Leave to _____

Item _____ Leave to _____

Item _____ Leave to _____

Item _____ Leave to _____

Item _____ Leave to _____

Item _____ Leave to _____

Item _____ Leave to _____

Item _____ Leave to _____

Item _____ Leave to _____

Item _____ Leave to _____

Item _____ Leave to _____

Item _____ Leave to _____

Item _____ Leave to _____

Item _____ Leave to _____

Item _____ Leave to _____

Item _____ Leave to _____

Item _____ Leave to _____

Item _____ Leave to _____

Item _____ Leave to _____

Item _____ Leave to _____

Item _____ Leave to _____

Item _____ Leave to _____

Item _____ Leave to _____

WISHES REGARDING PETS

Indicate who you would like to continue to care for your pets. Place any information about your pets in this section including name, year of birth, favorite foods, and any special care needs. Include the name, address, and phone number of the veterinarian and where records are located.

_____

_____

_____

_____

_____

_____

_____

_____

_____

_____

_____

_____

_____

_____

Chapter

XIV

SPECIAL MESSAGES

SPECIAL MESSAGES

This section is set aside to record special messages to family members and friends. Write the individual's name followed by your message. You may wish to sign and date each entry. Private messages may be sealed in the envelope located at the back of this book.

_____

_____

_____

_____

_____

_____

_____

_____

_____

_____

_____

_____

_____

Appendix

EXAMPLES OF OBITUARIES

This book is dedicated to the memory of Judge John S. Page, who died unexpectedly in January 1990. The following text is offered as a sample of a detailed obituary.

Judge John S. Page

Judge John S. Page, 67, of Stuart, Florida and formerly of Elgin, died on Monday, January 8, 1990, in Martin Memorial Hospital, Stuart, Florida.

Judge Page was born in Elgin, Illinois on January 26, 1922, the son of Judge Charles D. Page and Helen Starring Page. He attended Elgin Academy and received his bachelor's degree from the University of Michigan. During World War II he served in the Navy, primarily in the field of intelligence. Following discharge in 1946, he married Shirley Jessien, also of Elgin, and entered the University of Michigan Law School. He graduated in 1949.

In 1949, Judge Page established a law practice in Elgin. He was elected judge of the Elgin City Court in 1963 and subsequently became a judge of the Circuit Court in Geneva in that same year. He served as Chief Judge of the Circuit Court from 1970 through 1972. Judge Page served on the Elgin School Board for eight years, was a past exalted ruler of the Elgin Elks Lodge 737, and was a member of many other civic organizations in the Elgin area.

Judge Page retired in 1979, and he and Mrs. Page moved to Stuart, Florida in 1986. He is survived by his wife, Shirley Jessien Page; a son, Charles Page of Elgin; three daughters: Lucinda Knox, Tampa, FL; Sally Danzinger, Arlington Heights; Susan Chesbrough, Elgin, and seven grandchildren.

Services will be at 11 a.m. Friday at the Wait-Ross-Allanson Funeral Chapel, Elgin, the Rev. Willis A. Reed officiating. Visitation from 6-8 p.m. today in the funeral chapel. Private burial at Bluff City Cemetery.

SAMPLE OBITUARIES

John Doe

John Doe, 68, of Sandy Hills, died Friday at home. A native of Clear Rivers, Wisconsin, he had been a resident of Sandy Hills for seventeen years. He was a retired carpenter and a member of St. Andrew Presbyterian Church. He was also a member of the American Legion and the Lion's Club. He is survived by his wife, Emily; a son, Todd, of Louisville, KY; two brothers, Carl and Joe of Green Rivers, WI; and two grandchildren. Burns and Baums Funeral Home.

Joan Jarvis

Joan Jarvis, 58, of Pleasant Valley, died Saturday at South City Hospital. A native of Chicago, Illinois, she had been a resident of Pleasant Valley for twenty-two years. She was a division manager for Smith Furniture, a member of the Pleasant Valley Garden Club and the Pleasant Valley Women's League. She is survived by her husband, Henry; a son, Donald of New York City; three sisters, Betty, Judy, and Vivian of Chicago; and one grandson. Memorial Gardens Funeral Home.

Tony Joe Moritz

Tony Joe Moritz, 44, of Rock River, died Monday. A native of Sunny Beach, he had been a resident of Rock River for fifteen years. He was vice-president of finance for Jones Welker Corporation and a member of the American Association for Accountants, the Kiwanis, and treasurer of the Rock River Men's Bowling League. He is survived by his wife, Margery; four sons, Jeffrey, Ronald, Calvin, and Elliot, all of Rock River; his parents, Mr. and Mrs. Lloyd Moritz, of Sunny Beach; a sister, Rosemary, of Sunny Beach; and a brother, Theodore, of San Diego, CA. Smiley Funeral Home.

Chad Berger

Chad Berger, 36, of New York City, died Monday at City Hospital. He was a theatrical set designer, a published poet, and a member of Congregation Beth Israel. He is survived by his mother, Isabel; one brother, Kenneth, of New York City; and two nephews. Nesbaum Funeral Home.

THE FOLLOWING IS AN EXAMPLE OF A LIVING WILL FOR THE STATE OF FLORIDA. PLEASE CONTACT CHOICE IN DYING AT (800) 989-WILL TO RECEIVE A FREE COPY OF APPROPRIATE ADVANCE DIRECTIVES FOR YOUR STATE.

FLORIDA LIVING WILL

Declaration made this _____day of _____, 19____.

I, _____, willfully and voluntarily make known my desire that my dying not be artificially prolonged under the circumstances set forth below, and I do hereby declare:

If at any time I have a terminal condition and if my attending or treating physician and another consulting physician have determined that there is no medical probability of my recovery from such a condition, I direct that life-prolonging procedures be withheld or withdrawn when the application of such procedures would serve only to prolong artificially the process of dying, and that I be permitted to die naturally with only the administration of medication or the performance of any medical procedure deemed necessary to provide me with comfort care or to alleviate pain.

It is my intention that this declaration be honored by my family and physician as the final expression of my legal right to refuse medical or surgical treatment and to accept the consequences for such refusal.

In the event that I have been determined to be unable to provide express and informed consent regarding the withholding, withdrawal, or continuation of life-prolonging procedures, I wish to designate, as my surrogate to carry out the provisions of this declaration:

Name _____

Address _____

_____Zip Code_____

Phone_____

INSTRUCTIONS

PRINT THE DATE

PRINT YOUR NAME

PRINT THE NAME, HOME ADDRESS, AND TELEPHONE NUMBER OF YOUR SURROGATE

© 1993
CHOICE IN DYING, INC.

I wish to designate the following person as my alternate surrogate, to carry out the provisions of this declaration should my surrogate be unwilling or unable to act on my behalf:

Name _____

Address _____

_____Zip Code_____

Phone_____

Additional instructions (optional):

I understand the full import of this declaration, and I am emotionally and mentally competent to make this declaration.

Signed _____

Witness 1:

Signed _____

Address _____

Witness 2:

Signed _____

Address _____

Courtesy of Choice In Dying (11/93)
200 Varick Street, New York, NY 10014
800-989-9455

PRINT THE NAME, HOME ADDRESS, AND TELEPHONE NUMBER OF YOUR ALTERNATE SURROGATE

ADD PERSONAL INSTRUCTIONS (IF ANY)

SIGN THE DOCUMENT

WITNESSING PROCEDURE

TWO WITNESSES MUST SIGN AND PRINT THEIR ADDRESSES

© 1993
CHOICE IN DYING, INC.

ORGANIZATIONS

We have attempted to list potentially helpful organizations and to ensure that their names, addresses, and phone numbers are current and correct. Please contact the authors with any corrections, additional recommendations, or negative experiences for future editions.

Sorrow which is never spoken is the heaviest load to bear.

Samuel Butler

AIDS National Interfaith Network
110 Maryland Avenue N.W., Suite 504
Washington, DC 20002
(202) 546-0807

AIDS National Interfaith Network is a private, non-profit organization founded in 1988. This organization links people of faith, mobilizes religious leadership, promotes quality pastoral services, encourages culturally appropriate prevention education, and fosters provision of compassionate, nonjudgmental services to and advocacy on behalf of those infected and affected by HIV/AIDS.

American Association of Retired Persons
601 E Street N.W.
Washington, DC 20049
(202) 434-2277

AARP is the nation's largest and oldest organization of Americans aged 50 and older. AARP offers educational and community service programs, legislative representation, publications, and other direct member benefits. (*See* "Widowed Persons Service" *below.*)

Cemetery Consumer Service Council
P.O. Box 3574
Washington, DC 20007
(703) 379-6426

Handles general questions from consumers regarding problems in dealing with a cemetery or the purchase/performance of cemetery-related goods or services. Questions about gravesite memorials should be referred to (708) 869-2031.

Choice In Dying, Inc.
200 Varick Street
10th Floor
New York, NY 10014-4810
(800) 989-9455

Choice In Dying, Inc. is the nation's leading not-for-profit organization dedicated to protecting the rights and serving the needs of dying patients and their families. They advocate patients' rights to make their own decisions about medical treatment, and to receive compassionate and dignified care at the end of life. Choice In Dying provides statutory advance directives for each state free of charge, as well as other materials and services relating to end-of-life medical care. Callers can contact them toll free at 800-989-9455.

Compassionate Friends
P.O. Box 3696
Oak Brook, IL 60522-3696
(708) 990-0010

This is a self-help organization that offers friendship and understanding to bereaved parents and siblings, and may be of help to parents who have lost a child of any age. The national office assists in developing new chapters and offers consultation to existing chapters. The organization also has a list of books and brochures dealing with death and bereavement that may be ordered from the national office.

Cremation Association of North America
401 North Michigan Avenue
Chicago, IL 60611
(312) 644-6610
Request free pamphlets regarding cremation.

Displaced Homemakers Network
See Women Work! *below*

Funeral and Memorial Societies of America
6900 Lost Lake Road
Egg Harbor, WI 54209
(800) 458-5563

To receive information about non-profit memorial societies and simple, affordable funerals, send the association a self-addressed, stamped #10 envelope with a small contribution. For $2.00, you can also receive a price list of wholesale costs for a variety of caskets. For further information, call (414) 868-3136. You can also look in the Yellow Pages for more information.

Funeral Service Consumer Assistance Program
2250 East Devon Avenue, Suite 250
Des Plaines, IL 60018
(800) 662-7666

This is an independent, not-for-profit, charitable organization that researches and provides consumer information on death, grief, and funeral services. This organization will help you identify, address, and resolve complaints about a funeral service contract. Ask for these pamphlets: *A Consumer's Guide*, *Pre-need Funeral Planning*, *Planning a Funeral*, and *Understanding Grief*.

Hemlock Society U.S.A.
P.O. Box 11830
Eugene, OR 97440-3900
(503) 342-5748

This is a non-profit educational corporation that supports both passive and voluntary euthanasia. Its purpose is to modify the law, permitting a terminally ill person to take moral and legal responsibility for his or her death. The society also publishes books regarding this issue and has chapters located throughout the country.

Jewish Funeral Directors of America
399 East 72nd Street, Suite 3F
New York, NY 10021
(212) 628-3465

Members of this organization are located throughout the U.S., as well as in Montreal and Toronto, Canada. Most have grief counselors on staff or will provide information on available community bereavement counseling services. All members offer pre-need packages. Publications of this group include the following: *The Jewish Funeral Guide* (in English and Russian), *How to Explain Death to Children*, and *Jewish Funeral Etiquette*.

The Living Bank
P.O. Box 6725
Houston, TX 77265
(800) 528-2971

Contact the Living Bank for organ donor forms.

Memorial Societies.
See Funeral and Memorial Societies of America.

National Association of People with AIDS
1413 K Street N.W.
Washington, DC 20005
(202) 898-0414

A non-profit organization that provides referrals to local support groups and information and educational resources for people living with AIDS. Operates a fax on demand service, (202) 789-2222, which covers a variety of issues related to AIDS.

National Association of Uniformed Services
  and Society of Military Widows
5535 Hampstead Way
Springfield, VA 22151
(703) 750-1342

This group offers support and assistance for widows and widowers of members of all branches of the military.

National Funeral Directors Association
11121 West Oklahoma Avenue
Milwaukee, WI 53227
(414) 541-2500
Offers free pamphlets regarding funeral services.

The National Hospice Organization
1901 North Moore Street, Suite 901
Arlington, VA 22209
(800) 658-8898

The purpose of hospice is to provide support and care for people in the final phase of a terminal disease so that they can live as fully and comfortably as possible. This organization is a national clearinghouse for locating hospice programs and information about hospice care. It also provides educational programs, publications, and referral services.

National Institute for Jewish Hospice
247 East Tahquitz Canyon Way, Suite 21
Palm Springs, CA 92262
(800) 446-4448; in California (213) 467-7423

This organization serves as a resource center that seeks to help terminal patients and their families deal with their grief by providing information about traditional Jewish views about death, dying, and managing the loss of a loved one.

Older Women's League
National Office
666 11th Street N.W., Suite 700
Washington, DC 20001
(202) 783-6686

Goals of the League include mutual support, achieving economic and social equity, and improving the image and status of older women. There are local chapters in more than half the states. Workshops are sponsored on such topics as employment of older women, health issues, and social security. OWL also offers relevant mail-order publications.

Parents Without Partners
401 North Michigan Avenue
Chicago, IL 60611-4267
(312) 644-6610

This is an educational organization devoted to the welfare and interests of single parents and their children. There are chapters in all 50 states that offer educational programs and discussion groups, recreational activities for children at low cost, social activities for adults, community service, and advocacy projects.

Self-Help Clearing House
Saint Clares-Riverside Medical Center
Denville, NJ 07834
(201) 625-7101

Ask for *The Self-Help Source Book*, which lists by category the self-help groups throughout the United States. This would be useful if you would like to join or start a support group.

Society for the Right to Die
See Choice In Dying.

T.H.E.O.S. (They Help Each Other Spiritually)
717 Liberty Avenue
1301 Clark Building
Pittsburgh, PA 15222-3510
(412) 471-7779

Network of local groups to assist young and middle-aged widowed people and their families to rebuild their lives through mutual self-help. Religious emphasis.

Widowed Persons Service
AARP
Social Outreach and Support
601 E Street N.W.
Washington, DC 20049
(202) 434-2260

One-to-one peer support for widows and widowers, run in cooperation with AARP and local community groups. There is an outreach service, which provides volunteers who are widowed to visit the newly bereaved and group meetings for discussion and mutual assistance. They also provide free booklets, referral services, manuals on starting support groups, and public education.

Women Work! National Network for Women's Employment
   (formerly Displaced Homemakers Network)
1625 K Street N.W., Suite 300
Washington, DC 20006
(202) 467-6346

Two-thirds of displaced homemakers are widows. This group offers career exploration, job readiness training, educational opportunities, and support groups. Goals include increasing options for self-sufficiency, and providing information about public policy issues which affect displaced homemakers. Write or call for a list of publications.

RECOMMENDED LEGAL AND FINANCIAL READINGS

Listed below is a sampling of the many books available in the legal and financial areas. Topics covered include estate planning, preparing a will and a living will, establishing trusts, information about social security, explaining probate, and describing the role of the executor or personal representative. Books on these subjects are constantly being revised and updated. See the legal reference section of your local bookstore or library for additional resources.

Look well into thyself; there is a source of strength which will always spring up if thou wilt always look there.

Marcus Aurelius

Abts, Henry W. III, *The Living Trust*. Chicago: Contemporary Books, 1993.

Appel, Jens C. III, and Gentry, F. Bruce, *The Complete Will Kit*. New York: John Wiley and Sons, 1990.

Bove, Alexander A. Jr., *The Complete Book of Wills and Estates*. New York: Henry Holt and Company, 1991.

Clifford, Denis, *Make Your Living Trust*. Berkeley, CA: Nolo Press, 1993.

Clifford, Denis, *Nolo's Simple Will Book*. 2d ed. Berkeley, CA: Nolo Press, 1994.

Clifford, Denis, *Plan Your Estate*. 3d ed. Berkeley, CA: Nolo Press, 1994.

Dowd, Merle E., *Estate Planning Made Simple*. New York: Doubleday, 1991.

Hauser, Thomas, *The Family Legal Companion*. New York: Allworth Press, 1992.

Jehle, Faustin F., *The Complete Guide to Social Security and Medicare*. Charlotte, VT: Williamson Publishing Company, 1990.

Larsen, David C., *You Can't Take It with You: A Step-by-step, Personalized Approach to Your Will to Avoid Probate and Estate Taxes*. New York: Vintage Books, 1988.

Manning, Jerome A., *Estate Planning: How to Preserve Your Estate for Your Loved Ones*. New York: Practicing Law Institute, 1992.

Plotnick, Charles K. and Leimberg, Stephen R., *The Executor's Manual: Everything You Need to Know to Handle an Estate*. New York: Doubleday, 1986.

Regan, John J. with Legal Council for the Elderly, *Your Legal Rights in Later Life*. Glenview, IL: Scott, Foresman and Company, 1989.

Sitarz, Daniel, *Prepare Your Own Will*. Carbondale, IL: Nova Publishing Company, 1991.

Soled, Alex J., *The Essential Guide to Wills, Estates, Trusts, and Death Taxes*. Glenview, IL: Scott, Foresman and Company, 1988.

Williams, Philip, *The Living Will and Durable Power of Attorney for Health Care Book*. Oak Park, IL: P. Gaines Company, 1991.

Williamson, Gordon, *Your Living Trust: How to Protect Your Estate from Probate, Taxes, and Lawyers*. New York: Perigree Books, 1992.

RECOMMENDED READINGS FOR SURVIVORS

Practical Information and Advice

Everyone can master a grief but he that has it.

Shakespeare

Anderson, Patricia, *Affairs in Order: A Complete Resource Guide to Death and Dying*. New York: MacMillan Publishing Company, 1991.

How to plan before one's death; how to deal with imminent death; and how to cope as a survivor with financial, legal, and bereavement issues after a loved one's death.

Becker, Marilyn R., *Preparing for a Parent's Death*. Oakland, CA: New Harbinger Publications, Inc., 1992.

This is an excellent resource guide for dealing with a parent's death. The author relates her experiences and those of others, including chapters that deal with talking to your parent about death, helping to choose care options, trying to involve your parent in making funeral and other necessary arrangements, and what to expect at the moment of actual death. This is a very compassionate and honest book.

Caine, Lynn, *Being a Widow*. New York: Viking Penguin, 1990.

A "self-help" book for widows. Speaks to the emotional and practical problems widows face, including financial, insurance-related, and legal.

Carlson, Lisa, *Caring for Your Own Dead*. Hinesburg, VT: Upper Access Publishers, 1987.

For those who wish to handle funeral arrangements themselves, including disposition of the body. Includes laws, regulations, and services available in each state, notes on body and organ donation, and the experiences of three persons who each planned and carried out a relative's funeral.

Carroll, David, *Living with Dying: A Loving Guide for Family and Friends*. New York: Paragon House, 1991.

Includes information on home care, rights of the patient, hospice care, funeral or memorial service arrangements, and bereavement.

Cohen, Donna and Eisdorfer, Carl, *Seven Steps to Effective Parent Care: A Planning and Action Guide for Adult Children with Aging Parents*. New York: A Jeremy P. Tarcher Book/Putnam Book, 1993.

A resource book for adults caring for aging parents that helps the reader evaluate and cope with potential frustrations and problems. Chapter Seven contains a "Values History Form," a tool that helps adults and their parents to approach many difficult and painful issues including attitudes toward illness, death, and dying. The authors also list selected readings and local, state, and national organizations that provide related information and services.

Cole, Diane, *After a Great Pain: A New Life Emerges*. New York: Summit Books, 1992.

Diane Cole's book deals with the loss of her mother, her husband's near-fatal bout with cancer, her own infertility, and her experience of being taken hostage for 39 hours. She describes how she dealt with each painful ordeal and how she emerged as a stronger person. An excellent book for anyone who has had a loss or who faces a terminal illness.

Colgrove, Melba, Bloomfield, Harold L., and McWilliams, Peter, *How to Survive the Loss of a Love*. Los Angeles: Prelude Press, 1991.

Colgrove and Bloomfield have written short one-page "chapters," each dealing with an aspect of loss, grief, mourning, or recovering from a loss. Opposite each chapter page is a poem written by Peter McWilliams that reflects that chapter's theme. This book is easy to read and offers practical advice and comfort for survivors.

DiGiulio, Robert C., *Beyond Widowhood: From Bereavement to Emergence and Hope*. New York: The Free Press, a division of Macmillan Inc., 1989.

Written by a widower, includes chapters on bereavement, identity loss, re-forming one's identity, growing through and beyond widowhood, remarriage, and the value of support groups.

Donnelly, Katherine Fair, *Recovering from the Loss of a Child*. New York: Macmillan Publishing Company, Inc., 1982.

Has chapters on miscarriage, Sudden Infant Death Syndrome, dealing with the surviving siblings, and a list of organizations that can help bereaved families.

Donnelly, Katherine Fair, *Recovering from the Loss of a Parent*. New York: Berkeley Publishers, 1993.

Discusses the trauma of holidays and anniversaries, coping with the surviving parent, and the grieving process.

Donnelly, Katherine Fair, *Recovering from the Loss of a Sibling*. New York: Dodd, Mead and Company, Inc., 1988.

Siblings of all ages discuss their experiences in dealing with the loss of a brother or sister. Sibling survivors are sometimes called "forgotten grievers." This book is valuable both for bereaved parents who have surviving children and for siblings who need to know how others have coped in similar situations.

Donnelley, Nina Herrmann, *I Never Know What to Say: How to Help Your Family and Friends Cope with Tragedy*. New York: Ballantine, 1990.

Nina Donnelley is a trained hospital chaplain who draws upon her personal and professional experiences regarding the process of mourning and what friends can do to help the mourner.

Fisher, Ida and Lane, Byron, *The Widow's Guide to Life*. Englewood Cliffs, NJ: Prentice-Hall, Inc., 1981.

A valuable, practical book, written by a woman who has been widowed twice. A complete resource book for widows that will help you handle all of your personal affairs, provide support, and show you how to establish your new identity as a single woman. Includes especially good chapters on finances and insurance, health, life planning, and career planning.

Foehner, Charlotte and Cozart, Carol, *The Widow's Handbook: A Guide for Living*. Golden, CO: Fulcrum Publishing, 1988.

An excellent book, covering a wide range of topics. These include obtaining legal help and financial advice, applying for benefits, budgeting, automobile maintenance, being a single parent, and estate planning.

Grollman, Earl A., *Living When a Loved One Has Died*. Boston: Beacon Press, 1977.

A book in free verse form whose purpose is to help you to manage wisely the emotions of your grief and to challenge you to confront creatively the death of your beloved. The contents contain musings on "Shock," "Suffering," "Recovery," and "A New Life."

Grollman, Earl A., *Talking about Death: A Dialogue Between Parent and Child*. Boston: Beacon Press, 1991.

How to explain death to children. Includes a parent's guide, recommended readings, and recommended videos.

Grollman, Earl A., *What Helped Me When My Loved One Died*. Boston: Beacon Press, 1981.

Parents, children, spouses, and others relate their personal experiences with the death of someone close to them.

Kohn, Jane Burgess and Kohn, Willard K., *The Widower*. Boston: Beacon Press, 1978.

A widower's story: includes sections on how to adjust to being a single parent, re-entry into dating, and re-marriage.

Kramer, Herbert and Kramer, Kay, *Conversations at Midnight: Coming to Terms with Death and Dying*. New York: William Morrow and Company, Inc., 1993.

This is an inspiring and moving book consisting of Herbert Kramer's meditations regarding his imminent death from cancer, interspersed with dialogues between him and his wife, a social worker experienced in working with dying persons.

Krementz, Jill, *How it Feels When a Parent Dies*. New York: Alfred A. Knopf, 1988.

Children and teens share their experiences and feelings regarding the death of a parent.

Kubler-Ross, Elisabeth, *Death: The Final Stage of Growth*. Annapolis, MD: Touchstone Books, 1986.

Interviews with dying persons.

Kubler-Ross, Elisabeth, *On Death and Dying*. New York: Macmillan, 1991.

This classic describes the stages of the acceptance of death; how to deal with anger, grief, and guilt feelings; and describes the experiences of others.

LeShan, Eda, *When a Parent Is Very Sick*. New York: The Atlantic Monthly Press, 1986.

This is an excellent book written for children. Topics covered include how to deal with a parent's illness, how to live day to day with a sick parent, what happens if a parent dies, the many ways in which grief and mourning are manifested, and how children whose parents die can go on with their lives.

Lightner, Candy and Hathaway, Nancy, *Giving Sorrow Words: How to Cope with Grief and Get on with Your Life*. New York: Warner Books, Inc., 1990.

Candy Lightner, founder of the organization MADD (Mothers Against Drunk Driving), describes the accidental death of her daughter and how she dealt with her grief. The authors present helpful interviews with persons who have lost loved ones and with psychologists and psychiatrists who have studied grief.

Morgan, Ernest, *Dealing Creatively with Death: A Manual of Death Education and Simple Burial*. Burnsville, NC: Celo Press, 1988.

Mr. Morgan wrote this book after he chaired a Quaker committee to study how American funeral practices could be simplified and made more meaningful. This thought-provoking book includes discussions about death education, the hospice movement, special issues for AIDS patients, the right to refuse medical treatment, simple cremation and burial, and various "death ceremonies." He also gives examples of different types of funeral and memorial services. There is an appendix of relevant organizations, including information regarding hospices throughout the U.S., how to locate simple burial boxes, and—of special interest—sample funeral/memorial services, including music and readings used.

Neeld, Elizabeth Harper, *Seven Choices: Taking the Steps to New Life after Losing Someone You Love*. New York: Clarkson N. Potter, Inc., 1990.

This book is highly recommended. Dr. Neeld describes her husband's sudden death and relates her feelings and experiences to seven phases of grieving that she has identified. Dr. Neeld's honesty and compassion make this book extremely moving and helpful. As she states in her Prologue, "Even though we can do nothing about the loss itself, we can, through the choices we make now, create for ourselves a new future."

Nudel, Adele Rice, *Starting Over: Help for Young Widows and Widowers*. New York: Dodd, Mead and Company, Inc., 1986.

Deals with grieving, guilt, anger, and coping with loneliness. Discusses support groups, single parenting, depression, and many other relevant issues.

Rando, Therese A., G*rieving: How to Go On Living When Someone You Love Dies*. New York: Bantam Books, 1991.

The author, a clinical psychologist, describes the grieving process and how it affects different individuals. Chapter titles include "Grieving Different Forms of Death," "Grieving and Your Family" (loss of spouse, adult losing parent, adult losing sibling, loss of child, helping children cope with death and mourning), "Resolving Your Grief," and "Getting Additional Help." There is a resource list at the end of the book.

Schmidt, Judith Sara, *How to Cope with Grief*. New York: Ballantine Books, 1989.

Fifty-two short chapters, or "thoughts," regarding death, grief, and surviving. Schmidt writes from her own and others' experiences: "...the ways I have found from deep within my grieved heart and soul, from the ancient ways of my tradition, from loving ones showing me the paths back to living."

Staudacher, Carol, *Beyond Grief: A Guide for Recovering from the Death of a Loved One*. Oakland, CA: New Harbinger Publications, Inc., 1987.

A sensitive, thorough book covering all aspects of grief, how to survive different types of losses (e.g., loss of a child, loss of a parent, accidental death, suicide, etc.), and how to receive help and also how to provide help to others who are grieving. Contains many anecdotes.

Staudacher, Carol, *Men & Grief: A Guide for Men Surviving the Death of a Loved One, a Resource for Caregivers and Mental Health Professionals*. Oakland, CA: New Harbinger Publications, Inc., 1991.

An extremely helpful book dealing with the various grief responses of men and how these traditionally differ from women's responses, the specific losses men may experience, and how men can better release and deal with grief. Contains many anecdotes.

Sterns, Ann Kaiser, *Living Through Personal Crisis*. New York: Ballantine Books, 1985.

This book is about the small and large losses that people experience, including the loss of a loved one. She emphasizes the problems that unresolved pain brings and the importance of grieving and mourning.

Tatelbaum, Judy, *The Courage to Grieve: Creative Living, Recovery, and Growth Through Grief*. New York: HarperCollins, 1984.

The author shows the importance of the grieving process, the different phases of grief following the death of a loved one, and the use of grief and loss as a "turning point" and a transformation of one's life.

Tatelbaum, Judy, *You Don't Have to Suffer: A Handbook for Moving Beyond Life's Crises*. New York: HarperCollins, 1990.

Ms. Tatelbaum believes that how we suffer and how much we suffer is a personal choice, even when faced with terrible life experiences. This is an interesting, challenging concept; the author is convinced that we can choose whether to live "fully awake and alive to life or closed down and suffering."

Taves, Isabella, *The Widow's Guide*. New York: Schocken Books, 1981.

Contains useful advice on how to deal with grief, stress, finances, family, and getting back into the world.

Upson, Norma S., *When Someone You Love Is Dying*. New York: Simon and Schuster, Inc., 1986.

Chapters include "Emotions," "Options for Care," "Legalities and Decisions," and "Special Considerations" (including those relevant to nontraditional couples).

Viorst, Judith, *Necessary Losses*. New York: Ballantine Books, 1989.

A thought-provoking book about how we grow and change through the losses that are an inevitable and necessary part of life. The last section is entitled "Loving, Losing, Leaving, Letting Go."

Yates, Martha, *Coping: a Survival Manual for Women Alone*. Englewood Cliffs, NJ: Prentice-Hall, Inc., 1976.

Practical advice and tips for all areas of a newly widowed or divorced woman's life.

One generation passeth away, and another generation cometh: but the earth abideth forever.

Ecclesiastes

HIV/AIDS

The following publications would be of special interest to persons with AIDS and their friends and family.

Cox, Elizabeth, *Thanksgiving: An AIDS Journal*. New York: Harper and Row, 1990.

Moving, candid account of her husband's battle with AIDS and how it affected Cox and their young son.

Curry, Hayden, Clifford, Denis, and Leonard, Robin, *A Legal Guide for Lesbian and Gay Couples*. Berkeley, CA: Nolo Press, 1994.

This book discusses the legal status and laws pertaining to gay and lesbian couples in the United States. Includes bibliographical references and an index.

Donnelley, Katherine Fair, *Recovering from the Loss of a Loved One to AIDS: Help for Surviving Family, Friends, and Lovers Who Grieve*. New York: St. Martin's Press, 1994.

This highly recommended book deals with the special issues and concerns of persons who lose someone to AIDS. There are first-hand accounts by survivors, helpful advice given by bereavement counselors, and a resource list of support groups and relevant publications at the end of the book.

Kubler-Ross, Elisabeth, *AIDS: The Ultimate Challenge*. New York: Macmillan Publishing Company, Collier Books, 1993.

Dr. Kubler-Ross discusses the social and moral issues regarding AIDS and the way in which persons with AIDS can die with dignity, surrounded by their loved ones. The book includes chapters about women, children, and babies with AIDS.

Martelli, Leonard J., *When Someone You Know Has AIDS*. New York: Crown Publishers, Inc., 1993.

This book covers many areas, including facts about AIDS, legal and financial issues, how to obtain necessary help, problems that can occur in a relationship when one partner is ill, and ways that survivors can cope with their feelings of loss and grief. There is a directory of organizations, both national and state level, and a glossary of terms associated with AIDS.

Moffatt, Betty Clare, *When Someone You Love Has AIDS*. Santa Monica, CA: IBS Press, 1986.

Written by the mother of a person with AIDS.

Monette, Paul, *Borrowed Time: An AIDS Memoir*. New York: Harcourt, Brace, Jovanovich, 1988.

Paul Monette is a novelist and a poet who is gay. This is a beautifully written memoir about his partner, who contracted AIDS and subsequently died. This book eloquently portrays both the nature of the disease and its effects on persons with AIDS and their survivors.

Nungesser, Lon G. with Bullock, William D., *Notes on Living Until We Say Goodbye*. San Francisco: HarperSan Francisco, 1992.

The author writes from his own experiences with AIDS. Discusses how to deal with the stigma of the AIDS diagnosis and the rejection of others. Includes information on how to cope with your partner's feelings, with your own anger and depression, and with family relationships. Also discusses how to take responsibility for your own health care.

Individual Experiences of Bereavement

Blankenship, Jayne, *In the Center of the Night*. New York: G.P. Putnam's Sons, 1984.

Honest recounting of the feelings and experiences of a young widow and her son.

Brothers, Joyce, *Widowed*. New York: Simon and Schuster, 1990.

Dr. Brothers candidly describes her own experiences after the death of her husband. She discusses what helped her get through the first year of widowhood, what she would have done differently, and what advice she would offer to other persons who face the death of a loved one.

Caine, Lynn, *Widow*. New York: Bantam Books, 1987.

Highly recommended candid account. The author discusses her grief and anger, her financial troubles, problems with her young children, and her feelings about society's views of widows.

Coughlin, Ruth, *Grieving: A Love Story*. New York: Random House, 1993.

A beautifully written account of the author's devastation following her husband's death from cancer. "No one can tell you about grief, about its limitless boundaries....No matter how many times you hear the word 'final,' it means nothing until final is actually final."

Graham, Laurie, *Rebuilding the House: One Woman's Passage Through Grief*. New York: Viking Penguin Books, 1990.

After the death of her husband, the author struggles to restore their New Jersey farmhouse while trying to come to terms with her grief.

Gunther, John, *Death Be Not Proud*. New York: HarperCollins, 1987.

Very moving account about the illness and death of the author's son.

Hersey, Jean, *A Widow's Pilgrimage*. New York: The Seabury Press, 1979.

Contains the author's journal, kept just before her husband's sudden death until two-and-one-half years later.

Hosansky, Anne, *Widow's Walk: One Woman's Spiritual and Emotional Journey to a New Life*. New York: Donald I. Fine, Inc., 1993.

Highly recommended. Beautifully written, candid, moving, interspersed with humor, and very readable.

L'Engle, Madelaine, *Two-part Invention*. New York: Farrar, Straus and Giroux, 1988.

The history of the author's courtship with her husband alternates with chapters dealing with his illness and subsequent death. Very eloquent and deals honestly with the difficulties of living with a loved one who is dying.

Was ever grief like mine?

George Herbert

Lerner, Gerda, *A Death of One's Own*. Madison, WI: University of Wisconsin Press, 1985.
A moving account of her husband's eighteen-month illness and subsequent death.

Lewis, C.S., *A Grief Observed*. New York: Bantam Books, 1976.
Recounts Lewis' grief at the death of his wife and his struggle to regain his religious convictions.

Lindbergh, Anne Morrow, *Hour of Gold, Hour of Lead*. San Diego: HarBrace, 1993.
A sensitive account, through letters and a journal, of the kidnapping and death of the author's first child.

Schreiber, Le Anne, *Midstream: The Story of a Mother's Death and a Daughter's Renewal*. New York: Viking Penguin, 1991.
The author's journal kept during her mother's struggle with cancer. She writes candidly about the gamut of emotions she experienced and how each of the family members coped.

Taylor, Nick, *A Necessary End*. New York: Nan A. Talese/Doubleday, 1993.
Nick Taylor tells of an encounter we all dread but someday will contend with: seeing our parents to the end of their lives. Simply, honestly written. Describes his love for his parents—and also the annoyances he feels in dealing with some of their problems and the difficulties he faces after their deaths.

PERSONAL RECOMMENDATIONS

The following books provide interesting insights into the problems of being human. Personal choices are subjective and difficult to defend. A book that "speaks" to one person may not appeal to another. Each of the following books answered a strong personal need at one time or another, not necessarily regarding issues of grief or loss, but dealing in some way with the search for what "really matters" in life.

Some of these books have been critically acclaimed while others are not widely known. They are grouped below according to their main theme. We offer this list in the hope that other readers will also gain solace and insight from these authors' words.

Finding Meaning in Life

Campbell, Joseph, *Myths to Live By*. New York: Bantam Books, 1984.

Rilke, Rainer Maria, *Letters to a Young Poet*. New York: W.W. Norton and Company, 1963.

Watts, Alan W., *The Wisdom of Insecurity*. New York: Random House, 1968.

Interpersonal Relationships

Gaines, Charles, *A Family Place: A Man Returns to the Center of His Life*. New York: The Atlantic Monthly Press, 1994.

Lindbergh, Anne Morrow, *The Flower and the Nettle*. New York: HarBrace, 1993.

Lindbergh, Anne Morrow, *Locked Rooms and Open Doors*. New York: HarBrace, 1993.

Lindbergh, Anne Morrow, *War Within and Without*. New York: HarBrace, 1980.

Rogers, Carl and Stevens, Barry, *Person to Person: The Problem of Being Human*. Moab, Utah: Real People Press, 1967.

Stevens, Barry, *Don't Push the River*. Berkeley, CA: Celestial Arts, 1985.

The universe is change, life is understanding.

Marcus Aurelius

Aging

LeShan, Eda, *Oh, to Be 50 Again!: On Being Too Old for a Mid-life Crisis*. New York: Times Books/Random House, 1986.

Lessing, Doris, *The Summer Before the Dark*. New York: Random House, 1983.

Sarton, May, *Recovering*. New York: W.W. Norton and Company, 1987.

Sarton, May, *At Seventy*. New York: W.W. Norton and Company, 1993.

Sarton, May, *Journal of a Solitude*. New York: W.W. Norton and Company, 1992.

Sarton, May, *Endgame: Journal of the 79th Year*. New York: W.W. Norton and Company, 1992.

Dealing With Loss

L'Engle, Madeleine, *The Summer of the Great Grandmother*. New York: Harper-Collins, 1984.

Lindbergh, Anne Morrow, *Hour of Gold, Hour of Lead*. New York: HarBrace, 1993.

Reflections On Life

Gilman, Dorothy, *A New Kind of Country*. New York: Fawcett, 1989.

L'Engle, Madeleine, *A Circle of Quiet*. New York: HarperCollins, 1984.

Sarton, May, *The House by the Sea*. New York: W.W. Norton and Company, 1981.

Stoddard, Alexandra, *Making Choices: The Joy of a Courageous Life*. New York: William Morrow and Company, 1994.

QUOTES ABOUT LIFE

Our birth is but a sleep and a forgetting.
—*Wordsworth*

Have courage for the great sorrows of life and patience for the small ones.
—*Victor Hugo*

All life is an experiment. The more experiments you make the better.
—*Emerson*

Life is a comedy that the old have seen, and lived in.
—*Joseph Joubert*

Age is...the ripening, the swelling, of fresh life within, that withers and bursts the husk.
—*George Macdonald*

There is nothing permanent except change.
—*Heraclitus*

In every real man a child is hidden that wants to play.
—*Nietzsche*

I warmed both hands before the fire of life:
It sinks, and I am ready to depart.
—*Walter Savage Landor*

Life is half spent before we know what it is.
—*George Herbert*

To believe in immortality is one thing, but it is first needful to believe in life.
—*R.L. Stevenson*

Blessed is the generation in which the old listen to the young; and doubly blessed is the generation in which the young listen to the old.
—*The Talmud*

The universe is change, life is understanding.
—*Marcus Aurelius*

Live not as if you have ten thousand years before you.
—*Marcus Aurelius*

While the fates permit, live happily; life speeds on with hurried step, and with winged days the wheel of the headlong years is turned.
—*Seneca*

Apart from man, no being wonders at its own existence.
—*Arthur Schopenhauer*

He who asks of life nothing but the improvement of his own nature...is less liable than anyone to miss and waste life.
      —*Henri Frederic Amiel*

There is no wealth but life.
      —*John Ruskin*

May you live all the days of your life.
      —*Jonathan Swift*

Life can only be understood backwards; but it must be lived forwards.
      —*Kierkegaard*

...I shall not pass this way again.
      —*William Penn*

It is not death that man should fear, but he should fear never beginning to live.
      —*Marcus Aurelius*

Man was not born to solve the problems of the universe, but to put his finger on the problem and then to keep within the limits of the comprehensible.
      —*Goethe*

The unexamined life is not worth living.
      —*Socrates*

As soon as you trust yourself, you will know how to live.
      —*Goethe*

The web of our life is of a mingled yarn, Good and ill together.
      —*Shakespeare*

All say, "How hard it is that we have to die"—a strange complaint to come from the mouths of people who have had to live.
      —*Mark Twain*

Our lives resemble the Sibylline Books: the less there is left of it, the more precious it becomes.
      —*Goethe*

Death twitches my ear. "Live," he says; "I am coming."
      —*Virgil*

A useless life is an early death.
      —*Goethe*

Our life, a little gleam of time between eternities.
      —*Carlyle*

Abridge your hopes in proportion to the shortness of the span of human life...enjoy therefore the present time, and trust not too much what tomorrow may produce.
—*Horace*

Everyone is born a king, and most people die in exile.
—*Oscar Wilde*

Life is hardly more than a fraction of a second. Such a little time to prepare oneself for eternity!!!
—*Paul Gauguin*

Life is like playing a violin solo in public and learning the instrument as one goes on.
—*Samuel Butler*

To live is the rarest thing in the world. Most people exist, that is all.
—*Oscar Wilde*

QUOTES ABOUT TIME

Time does not become sacred to us until we have lived it.
—*John Burroughs*

Time is a river without banks.
—*Anonymous*

Wait for that wisest of all counselors, time.
—*Pericles*

O! Call back yesterday, bid time return.
—*Shakespeare*

No man is rich enough to buy back his past.
—*Oscar Wilde*

One generation passeth away, and another generation cometh: but the earth abideth forever.
—*Ecclesiastes*

Come what may, Time and the hour runs through the roughest day.
—*Shakespeare*

You can ask for anything you like, except time.
—*Napolean Bonaparte*

And time remembered is grief forgotten...
—*Swinburne*

Lost time is never found again.
—*Benjamin Franklin*

Nothing can bring back the hour
Of splendour in the grass, of glory in the flower.
  —*Wordsworth*

Time, like an ever-rolling stream, Bears all its sons away...
  —*Isaac Watts*

Time is flying never to return.
  —*Virgil*

Every man desires to live long; but no man would be old.
  —*Jonathan Swift*

Dost thou love life? Then do not squander time; for that's the stuff
life is made of.
  —*Benjamin Franklin*

To improve the golden moment of opportunity and catch the good that
is within our reach, is the great art of life.
  —*Samuel Johnson*

Time wasted is existence; us'd is life.
  —*Edward Young*

On the wings of time grief flies away.
  —*Jean de La Fontaine*

Time is but the stream I go a-fishing in.
  —*Thoreau*

The inaudible and noiseless foot of time.
  —*Shakespeare*

...there is nothing more fleeting than years.
  —*Ovid*

Winter is on my head, but eternal spring is in my heart...
  —*Victor Hugo*

...thinking of the days that are no more.
  —*Tennyson*

But at my back I always hear Time's winged chariot hurrying near...
  —*Andrew Marvell*

All my possessions for a moment of time.
  —*Elizabeth I Queen of England. Alleged last words.*

Time goes, you say? Ah, no! Alas, Time stays, we go.
  —*Austin Dobson*

Quotes About Death, Loss, and Remembrance

Death be not proud...
  —*John Donne*

Look well into thyself; there is a source of strength which will always
spring up if thou wilt always look there.
  —*Marcus Aurelius*

With rue my heart is laden
For golden friends I had,
For many a rose-lipt maiden
And many a lightfoot lad.
  —*A.E. Houseman*

No man is an island, entire of itself; every man is a piece of the
continent, a part of the main.
  —*John Donne*

Take away love and our earth is a tomb.
  —*Robert Browning*

Hope is a waking dream.
  —*Aristotle*

...thinking of the days that are no more.
  —*Tennyson*

Love is as strong as death.
  —*Solomon*

To lose a friend is the greatest of all losses.
  —*Publius Syrus*

Those who have endeavored to teach us to die well, have taught
few to die willingly.
  —*Samuel Johnson*

I have a rendezvous with death...
  —*Alan Seeger*

I want death to find me planting cabbages.
  —*de Montaigne*

No funeral gloom...when I am gone,
Corpse-gazings, tears, black rainment, graveyard, grimness.
  —*William Allingham*

Remember me when I have gone away,
Gone far into the silent land.
  —*Christina Rossetti*

Death,
The undiscover'd country, from whose bourn
No traveller returns.
   —*Shakespeare*

So may he rest; his faults lie gently on him!
   —*Shakespeare*

...Good night, sweet prince,
And flights of angels sing thee to thy rest!
   —*Shakespeare*

Because I could not stop for Death,
He kindly stopped for me...
   —*Emily Dickinson*

As men, we are all equal in the presence of death.
   —*Publius Syrus*

He was a man, take him for all in all,
I shall not look upon his like again.
   —*Shakespeare*

...even the weariest river, Winds somewhere safe to sea.
   —*Swinburne*

Death is a shadow that always follows the body.
   —*English Proverb*

I do not believe that any man fears to be dead,
but only the stroke of death.
   —*Francis Bacon*

The grave's a fine and private place,
But none, I think, do there embrace.
   —*Andrew Marvell*

We sometimes congratulate ourselves at the moment of waking
from a troubled dream; it may be so the moment after death.
   —*Nathaniel Hawthorne*

Death cancels everything but truth....
   —*William Hazlitt*

Quotes About Grief

All farewells should be sudden, when forever,
Else they make an eternity of moments,
And clog the last sad sands of life with tears.
  —*Lord Byron*

Was ever grief like mine?
  —*George Herbert*

Is there pity sitting in the clouds,
That sees into the bottom of my grief?
  —*Shakespeare*

Everyone can master a grief but he that has it.
  —*Shakespeare*

Those who do not feel pain seldom think that it is felt.
  —*Samuel Johnson*

People in distress never think that you feel enough.
  —*Samuel Johnson*

After great pain a formal feeling comes—
The nerves sit ceremonious like tombs...
  —*Emily Dickinson*

This is the hour of lead...
First chill, then stupor, then the letting go.
  —*Emily Dickinson*

Sorrow makes us all children again.
  —*Emerson*

Of all men's miseries the bitterest is this, to know so much
and to have control over nothing.
  —*Herodotus*

There is no greater sorrow than to recall, in misery, the time
when we were happy.
  —*Dante Alighieri*

While grief is fresh, every attempt to divert only irritates. You
must wait till it be digested...
  —*Samuel Johnson*

Being a man, ne'er ask the gods for a life set free from grief, but ask for courage
that endureth long.
  —*Menander*

Sorrow which is never spoken is the heaviest load to bear.
    —Samuel Butler

...But grief returns with the revolving year.
    —Shelley

Nature's law,
That man was made to mourn.
    —Robert Burns

But if the while I think on thee, dear friend,
All losses are restored and sorrows end.
    —Shakespeare

Beware of desperate steps; the darkest day,
Lived till tomorrow, will have passed away.
    —William Cowper

Endure, and save yourself for happier times.
    —Virgil

Never apologize for showing feeling. When you do so,
you apologize for truth.
    —Benjamin Disraeli

Grief is itself a med'cine.
    —William Cowper

It (friendship) redoubleth joys, and cutteth griefs in halves.
    —Francis Bacon

 APPENDIX

EPITAPHS

...it is a far, far, better rest that I go to, than I have ever known.
—*Charles Dickens*

Here he lies where he longed to be;
Home is the sailor, home from the sea,
And the hunter home from the hill.
—*R.L. Stevenson*

Here lies one whose name is writ in water.
—*Keats' Epitaph for himself*

Nothing of him doth fade,
But doth suffer a sea-change
Into something rich and strange.
—*Shakespeare (inscribed on Shelley's gravestone)*

Excuse my dust.
—*Dorothy Parker*

Against you I will fling myself, unvanquished and unyielding, O Death!
—*Virginia Woolf (chosen by her husband Leonard Woolf as her epitaph.)*

In my end is my beginning.
—*Mary Stuart (Mary Queen of Scots). Her motto.*

LIGHT-HEARTED QUOTES

Be sure to send a lazy man for the angel of death.
—*Jewish proverb*

What you leave at your death, let it be without controversy,
else the lawyers will be your heirs.
—*Sir Thomas Browne*

Come for your inheritance and you may have to pay for the funeral.
—*Yiddish proverb*

Each person is born to one possession which outlives all his others—
his last breath.
—*Mark Twain*

The reports of my death are greatly exaggerated.
—*Mark Twain*

We die only once, and for such a long time!
—*Moliere*

If fame is to come only after death, I am in no hurry for it.
—*Marcus Valerius Martial*

Why is it we rejoice at a birth and grieve at a funeral? It is because we are not the person involved.
—*Mark Twain*

Life's too short for chess.
—*H.J. Byron*

I should have no objection to go over the same life from its beginning to the end; requesting only the advantage authors have, of correcting in a second edition the faults of the first.
—*Benjamin Franklin*

I feel no pain dear mother now, But oh, I am so dry!
O take me to a brewery, And leave me there to die.
—*Anonymous*

Life. A spiritual pickle preserving the body from decay.
—*Ambrose Bierce*

Unusual Funeral or Burial Ideas

The following unique options have been reported in the media and may offer a starting point for your own creative planning.

A California business offers a six-minute video tribute program. The video combines photographs of the deceased with various nature scenes and music. It can be played during the funeral/memorial service.

An Illinois pet cemetery allows pet owners who purchase a plot for their pet to have their ashes buried next to their animal, free of charge.

A Florida resident is having a mausoleum built that will eventually house his wife, himself—and his beloved DeLorean car.

Rental caskets are now available which have removable interiors—each with a different design, such as flags, wedding bands, or a golfing, farming, or fishing motif.

Burial-at-sea services can be purchased in many areas.

Cryogenic suspension is already available in some states. The best known may be Alcor Life Extension Foundation located in Scottsdale, Arizona. For further information, read *Affairs In Order*, listed in the "Recommended Readings for Survivors" section.

It was reported that a man who loved target shooting and a "good joke" specified that his ashes be placed in 20-gauge shells and shot in a volley by his friends over one of his favorite sites.

Some terminally ill persons may choose to hold commemorative services prior to death, which they attend.

At the gravesite, a friend could read a summary of your personal history from childhood on. You may want to write this yourself or the text could come from the material you include in Chapter II and on page 74 in Chapter VIII.

The cremated remains of a Pennsylvania resident were buried in the driver's seat of his 1984 Corvette. The car filled four cemetery plots.

A man planned a yacht cruise for all of his friends to take place after his death—complete with a jazz band and refreshments. His ashes were scattered during the cruise.

A baseball fan arranged to be buried in her favorite ball club's uniform. "Take Me Out to the Ballgame" was played during the service.

A soap opera fan was buried with a portable TV tuned to her favorite soaps channel.

In San Francisco, a columbarium uses unusual containers to store cremains, including cookie jars, cameras, and tobacco humidors.

A casket manufacturer in Tennessee makes coffins decorated with logos of major universities.

Headstones can be carved with a person's likeness or with something that symbolizes a hobby or interest. Examples include a fish with a lure in its mouth, a golf cart, sports car, boat, pet, home, or flower. Also, some headstones have color photos of the deceased embedded in them.

This is the ultimate "do-it-yourself" project. Al Carpenter, owner of Direct Funeral Services in Alameda, CA, will send you detailed plans for making your own casket. Mr. Carpenter states that "by building our own caskets, we are taking steps to de-institutionalize the funeralization business." He claims that a cemetery must accept a "home-made" casket and cannot charge a handling fee. Mr. Carpenter goes on to say that "no matter what carpentry skills you possess, you are going to turn out a beautiful work of art." For those making a casket for "future use," he suggests that it can be used in the interim as a coffee table (attach legs), a toy chest or hope chest, or as a bookcase or hutch after shelves are installed.

To order a set of plans, send a check or money order for $9.95 to:

> Al Carpenter
> Funeral Director
> Direct Funeral Services
> 1516 Oak Street, Suite 208
> Alameda, CA 94501
> (510) 865-3435

John Chew and his staff state that they are the only certified mummifiers in the U.S. They train their students at Lynn University (Boca Raton, FL) in traditional mortuary science and in the art of mummification. This process is described as the only permanent preservation of the body available. Mr. Chew and his program have been the subject of many news articles and several TV shows.

Graduates of the program become agents for Summum, a non-profit organization based in Utah. Prospective clients, over 135 persons to date, usually purchase life insurance policies to cover the cost of the eventual mummification process. Prices can range from $7,000 to $150,000, depending on the type of "container" and mausoleum chosen.

For further information, contact:

> Summum
> 707 Genesee Avenue
> Salt Lake City, UT 84104
> (801) 355-0137

INDEX

ABOUT THE AUTHORS

The authors began writing *Last Wishes* more than ten years ago. The death of a close relative, and the difficulties of searching for each necessary document and planning the funeral without knowing the deceased person's preferences, motivated completion of the book.

Lucinda Page Knox holds a master's degree in social work from the University of Michigan and is a member of the Academy of Certified Social Workers. Part of her career has been spent working with dying patients in an acute care hospital. She is currently president of Applied Science Corporation in Tampa, Florida.

Michael D. Knox has a Ph.D. in psychology from the University of Michigan. He is professor and chairman of the Department of Community Mental Health at the University of South Florida. He holds a joint appointment as professor of Medicine in the Department of Internal Medicine at the USF College of Medicine. Dr. Knox also serves as director of the USF Center for HIV Education and Research and is a fellow of both the American Psychological Association and the American Psychological Society.

The following envelope contains sealed instructions and requests to be opened upon my death.

This envelope is designed for any special instructions that you may wish to be sealed until your death.